33288085987305

D1058715

Instant

Influence

Instant

Influence

How to Get Anyone to Do Anything — *Fast*

Michael V. Pantalon, PhD

Little, Brown and Company
New York Boston London

Little, Brown and Company
Hachette Book Group
237 Park Avenue, New York, NY 10017
www.hachettebookgroup.com

First Edition: May 2011

Little, Brown and Company is a division of Hachette Book Group, Inc. The Little, Brown name and logo are trademarks of Hachette Book Group, Inc.

The publisher is not responsible for websites (or their content) that are not owned by the publisher.

Library of Congress Cataloging-in-Publication Data
Pantalon, Michael V.
    Instant influence : how to get anyone to do anything—fast /
Michael V. Pantalon. — 1st ed.
        p. cm.
    ISBN 978-0-316-08334-8
    1. Influence (Psychology)   2. Persuasion (Psychology)   3. Change (Psychology)
I. Title.
    BF774.P36 2011
    153.8'52—dc22   2010038836

10 9 8 7 6 5 4 3 2 1

RRD-IN

Printed in the United States of America

To my family—
my wife, Marianne Sharsky Pantalon, PhD,
and my sons, Matthew and Nicholas.
You inspire, motivate, and influence me
in all the best possible ways every day. I love you.

To everyone who continues to believe,
no matter what, that we might always be able
to influence ourselves and others for good.

Follow that will and that way which experience confirms to be your own.

—*Carl Jung*

Contents

Instant

Influence

Introduction:
Instant Influence in Action

The General Electric executives stared back at me, skeptical, unsettled. I couldn't blame them: these human resources specialists were all comfortable with their own procedures for dealing with difficult employees, but now they were being required to learn my approach as well. This training session was mandatory, and I could read opposition in their tightly folded arms and in the grim expressions on their faces. *I might have to be here,* their body language said, *but I sure don't have to like it.*

If I didn't quickly grab their attention, they might not be convinced that my technique for dealing with unmotivated workers was worth their while. I had them for only a few hours, and teaching them how to use this new approach would take every bit of that time. But if I spent all morning talking and they didn't participate, what good would that do?

Well, my method *is* called Instant Influence, and one of its most exciting features is that it can work almost immediately, often in seven minutes or less. What if I spent seven minutes motivating these executives to listen to my presentation?

WHAT IS INSTANT INFLUENCE?

As a psychologist and researcher at Yale, I've spent many years investigating ways to move people from feeling resistant to being motivated. I began by working with a technique developed by William R. Miller and Stephen Rollnick known as motivational interviewing,[1] but I found a way to take it further.[2] Over the past fifteen years, I've devised a groundbreaking six-step version that's so fast and so effective that it actually results in *instant* influence.

Instant Influence is the only scientifically proven method for motivating people in seven minutes or less. It gets people to take action by encouraging them to find their own reasons for doing what you are asking of them. Just by asking someone six simple questions, you can inspire him to realize why he might want to take some kind of action: quit smoking, get to work on time, fill out his quarterly reports, or pay you back that twenty dollars he owes you. Instant Influence works on pretty much anything at all. You can also use this approach on yourself, to become more productive, stick to your diet, take up exercise, or accomplish anything else you may be struggling with. It works on people who know they want to change and are eager to get started, people who think they want to change but fear they can't, and people who think they *don't* want to change. It doesn't really matter who uses it—Instant Influence just works.

The two greatest advantages of Instant Influence are that you can learn the technique quickly and see results almost immediately.[3] I developed it at the request of busy emergency room doctors seeking to motivate patients who came into the ER because of alcohol-related accidents and medical problems. They wanted to inspire these people to seek help for their drinking, but the only time the doctors had to reach them was while treating them in the ER. In other words, the doctors had about seven minutes to influence semi-inebriated patients who didn't necessarily view themselves as needing help.

Seven minutes, resistant patients, and a hectic emergency room. What could possibly move people to change their lives under those circumstances? The answer is simple: *their own reasons*. People usually act for their own reasons, not someone else's reasons. If they do change a behavior because of something someone else has said, most of the time that change won't stick. The secret of Instant Influence is that it helps people discover their own reasons for doing something, even something they thought they didn't want to do.

You help people not by telling them why they should change but, rather, by asking them why they might want to change. Here are the six steps that will allow you to achieve Instant Influence:

Step 1: Why might you change? (Or to influence yourself, why might I change?)

Step 2: How ready are you to change — on a scale from 1 to 10, where 1 means "not ready at all" and 10 means "totally ready"?

Step 3: Why didn't you pick a lower number? (Or if the influencee* picked 1, either ask the second question again, this time about a smaller step toward change, or ask, what would it take for that 1 to turn into a 2?)

Step 4: Imagine you've changed. What would the positive outcomes be?

Step 5: Why are those outcomes important to you?

Step 6: What's the next step, if any?

---

* Because we are talking about influence, and because "person whom you are trying to influence" seemed like an impossibly awkward phrase, I have used the term *influencee* throughout this book.

The ER docs were so successful using my approach that they were able to achieve a nearly 50 percent reduction in drinking among their "alcohol-involved" patients—just from seven-minute conversations. As a result, Instant Influence is now a standard part of care in emergency rooms and in major trauma units across the United States, and medical residents nationwide are required to learn it.

After I developed this technique, I went on to apply it in many other settings. I've introduced Instant Influence to professionals at all levels, from middle managers, sales representatives, and human resource specialists to CEOs. I've trained and coached key staff and executives at such companies as Bayer, Bristol-Myers Squibb, and General Electric, and at such training centers as the American Management Association and the Addiction Technology Transfer Center. I've worked with Ivy League universities, including Yale, Harvard, and Brown; such major federal agencies as the National Institutes of Health and the US Department of Health and Human Services; such prominent medical centers as Yale-New Haven Hospital, Harvard's McLean Hospital, and NY Langone Medical Center; and numerous state judicial branches and departments of probation and parole. I've trained staff from prominent drug and alcohol rehab centers, including Hazelden, Betty Ford, and Crossroads at Antigua. I've taught Instant Influence to healthcare providers, social workers, psychologists, psychiatrists, and case managers for the homeless, as well as teachers and parents.

After more than fifteen years of training, research, and hands-on coaching experience, I know that Instant Influence can work on virtually anyone, from the most motivated CEO to the most resistant teenager.[4] The technique works well with colleagues, loved ones, even strangers. You can also use Instant Influence to help yourself achieve any type of goal, from improving job performance, negotiating contracts, and boosting sales to following through on weight loss and exercise plans, giving up cigarettes, and resolving problems in personal relationships.

LETTING PEOPLE CONVINCE THEMSELVES

Since people respond much better when they act for their own reasons rather than yours, we need to help them discover their reasons as soon as possible. However, if you're working with people who are resistant, as I was with the GE group, acknowledging that resistance—instead of fighting it—is a surprisingly effective way of getting them to be less defensive and more open.

Of course, that's easier said than done, especially when fifty underwhelmed pairs of eyes are glaring at you. But I had faith in this approach, so I forged ahead with my group of reluctant GE executives.

"Hey," I said as calmly as I could. "I know none of you really chose to be here. And you may not want to hear about yet another 'fantastic' method from yet another Ivory Tower egghead." I wanted to sincerely acknowledge their resistance and to do something known in motivation research as "denigrating the messenger." Both are important techniques for reinforcing an influencee's autonomy.

As I'd hoped, my self-deprecation got some laughs, and I could see the managers looking at one another in surprise. My frank acknowledgment of their point of view, rather than an attempt to sell them on mine, was the last thing they expected.

"So," I continued, "why are you here?"

The slight positive response I had won was instantly gone. "We're here because we *have* to be," one woman said, enunciating each word with exaggerated patience.

"Really? So every HR executive is here? Every single one?"

This got a few laughs. "Well, not Frank," one man said.

"He always finds an out. What is it this time—a dental appointment?"

"All right, then," I said. "You could have found some way to blow off this meeting, like Frank did, but you didn't. So tell me. Why are you here?"

I had just used Step 1: Why might you change? (Or, in this case, why have you changed?) Grudgingly, the executives began to give their answers. "Because we care about this company, and we want it to do well." "My boss asked me to attend, and I respect her, I guess." "I don't want to seem uncooperative."

Good responses, maybe, but they were still too vague to move anybody to action. If these people were going to change, they would need to find more personal reasons.

"Okay," I said. Time for Step 2: How ready are you to change—on a scale from 1 to 10, where 1 means "not ready at all" and 10 means "totally ready"? As always, I tailored my language to the people involved and the setting, making it more colloquial: "On a scale of 1 to 10, where 1 is 'not ready at all' and 10 is 'completely ready,' how ready are you to listen to my presentation today?"

The executives looked at one another, rolling their eyes. "Maybe a 3," a woman said finally. I could hear murmurs of agreement around the room.

"Great," I said, moving on to Step 3: Why didn't you pick a lower number? "You picked 3. Why didn't you choose a lower number?" Why, in other words, hadn't the woman described herself as being even *less* motivated? Why hadn't she chosen 2 or even 1 rather than 3?

This is the question that catches everybody off guard. They expect me to ask, why didn't you make it a higher number? In other words, why aren't you *more* motivated? Why don't you want more of what *I* think you should want?

But I hadn't asked that. Instead, I'd asked why her motivation was as high as it was. Why were they willing to listen to my presentation? Why were they here?

I had to wait a little while, but finally I got an answer. "Because even though I really believe in the way we do things now," one man said, "and even though I helped to refine our current procedures myself—and I *know* they work—even with all that, there are some employees we just don't know what to do with. Maybe this other approach might work with, say, one guy. That's why I'm here."

There were some nods and hints of agreement, but I still didn't think the room was totally with me. You can stop the Instant Influence process at any point when you think the other person is ready to change, but it's important not to stop *before* he's ready.

So on to Step 4: Imagine you've changed. What would the positive outcomes be? I hunted for a way to reword the question to fit this situation. "Look," I finally said. "I think it will go better for all of us if we spend just one more moment thinking about why you—not me, not your bosses, but you—might *ever* want to use this approach. I have my reasons for believing in it, but my reasons don't matter, because I'm not going to be dealing with your employees. You are. Suppose you've already adopted my methods. Just imagine for a moment that it's already done. What good could possibly come from that?"

There was a long, thoughtful silence. Then, from the back of the room, a middle-aged man spoke up, someone the organizers had warned me would be difficult to win over.

"You know," he said slowly, "when I was a kid, I wasn't exactly an A student. In fact, what I had then, they probably would call some form of ADHD today. I could never get myself to pay attention in class. I just didn't care enough.

"There was this one teacher, though, who really believed in me. She really went that extra mile to find out what I did care about, and somehow that got to me. Not what I was supposed to do. What I *cared* about."

He paused. "If it hadn't been for her, I might not have made it through high school."

He paused again. "If this method is anything like that, and it sounds like it is, maybe we should give it a try."

This man was an award-winning executive who clearly had the respect of his superiors and peers. But beyond his credentials, I could see that what had affected the rest of the people in the room most was how personally he had spoken. Somehow, we had left the realm of "I'm supposed to" or "My boss wants me to" and had entered a more meaningful place, one in which people were exploring their own reasons for listening to the presentation. As a result, in less than seven minutes, this man had gone from being extremely skeptical of my approach to giving a more effective speech about why he and his colleagues should listen closely than I could have ever scripted.

As often happens with Instant Influence, he had actually jumped ahead and completed one of the steps before I'd even had a chance to introduce it, in this case, Step 5: Why are those outcomes important to you? The man who had spoken up was imagining how he might be able to reach troubled employees, something that mattered to him because of how much he valued his teacher's efforts to get through to him when he was in school. I could see that the other executives were thinking hard, perhaps about people in their lives who had helped them or perhaps about all the seemingly unreachable people whom they might now be able to help. At this point, they had truly made it personal. They were thinking about their own reasons for change.

The time had come for Step 6: What's the next step, if any? But before I got the words out, the same executive beat me to it once again. "Okay, Dr. Pantalon," he said. "Why don't you go ahead and give us the presentation. We all have a job to do today, so let's get started."

I looked around the room. Instead of being stone-faced and slumped back in their chairs, the managers were leaning forward, eager, alert. They might not have been totally sold on the idea of my program, but at least now they were willing to listen. In less than seven minutes, they had moved from strong resistance to a willingness to take the first step toward change, but it wasn't because I had convinced them. They had found a way to convince themselves.

THE POWER OF *WHY*

In less than seven minutes, Instant Influence can get a person to agree to change. Actually implementing that change may take longer. But by the time the Instant Influence conversation has ended, the process will already be under way. The influencee will have begun to consider why she wants to change and, often without even realizing it, will be preparing to make changes. By getting in touch with her own powerful reasons to change, she plants seeds in fertile soil. You can't see the first stages of growth because they take place underground. Sooner or later, though, a tiny shoot will poke through to the daylight — and all because you had that first, seminal conversation.

Of course, sometimes Instant Influence doesn't work. If a person is deeply committed to refusing change, no motivational technique will make a difference. When someone genuinely doesn't want to change, change won't happen.

But far more often, even the most disaffected employee, the most reluctant client, the most negative teenager, the most adamant spouse, has a tiny spark of hope somewhere deep inside, a desire to reach common ground. If that spark is there, however small, Instant Influence can help you fan it into a glowing flame, either producing immediate action or opening up new possibilities for the long term. If you master the process and

11

stick with it, Instant Influence will help you get as far as is humanly possible.

My father was the first person to show me how many profound changes we can make in our lives when we're truly motivated. Although he was just twenty-three years old and spoke no English, he decided that he would leave his native Croatia to build a new life for himself in what must have seemed a completely strange new world, the United States. He began his long, difficult journey in 1962 as a stowaway on a train, trekked across four European countries on foot, and lived for several weeks in Paris under a bridge near the Seine. Eventually, in 1965, he reached the United States, a country where he knew no one.

What kept my father going? His dogged belief in his reasons for taking action. He knew why he wanted to escape a country with limited opportunities and why he wanted to make a new life, and so, against staggering odds, he somehow found a way to do it.

Significantly, whenever I ask my father how he was able to achieve his goal, he answers, "I don't know." Even though he succeeded long ago, the how question leaves us both with a feeling that what he had sought to do had been impossible. But when I ask my father why he wanted to leave Croatia, he always answers, "To be free." His reasons were so personal and so powerful that they enabled him to overcome every obstacle.

I once asked my father whether he thought he had been a little foolhardy. "Well, Michael," he answered, "if I had stopped to think about how absolutely crazy the whole idea was, I wouldn't have done it." Lucky for my family, my father never did focus on the how. Instead, he stayed focused on the why. Because his reasons were so clear to him, his motivation was strong. As a result, he was able to make his dream come true.

I've never faced hardships like my father's. But I've worked with people who have: at-risk teenagers, desperate psychiatric patients, people dependent on drugs and alcohol struggling to free themselves from their addictions. I've also trained many who deal with people in difficult situations: counselors working in teen group homes, parole officers supervising released prisoners, ER doctors dealing with drunk drivers. What I've learned from my work is that *why* may be the most powerful question on earth. Whether you're highly motivated or despairing of ever reaching your goal, finding that tiny spark of why you want to change can ultimately enable you to transform your life.

Most of us don't have my father's motivation. Luckily, most of us don't need it. *Instant Influence* can help any one of us take that critical first step toward change. What happens after that can be truly remarkable.

PART I

Get Anyone to Do Anything — *Fast*

CHAPTER ONE

What Makes People Want to Change?

Y ou've just left the gym to join your friend Kelly for coffee. When you meet up with her, she glances at your gym bag. "Oh," she says, "I wish I could be disciplined like you are. I never seem to get to the gym—I haven't exercised in months."

Being a good friend, you'd like to help, so you start trying to motivate Kelly to exercise. "It's so important," you say. "You'll look better. You'll feel better. You'll live longer..."

"I know," Kelly says. "Wouldn't that be nice! I just can't seem to get started."

"Starting can be tough," you say sympathetically. "But you'll feel so good afterward. You'll have lots of extra energy to get everything done."

"Maybe. I'm just always so tired."

"But exercise perks you up," you say. "I know. I'm always tired, too, but then I start my workout, and pretty soon I'm wide awake."

"You're so lucky. You're really disciplined. I'm just not."

Suddenly, you think you've come up with a perfect way to fix the whole problem. "Why don't you book some sessions with a personal trainer? That's how I got started. I thought it would be really expensive, but actually it's not. Then you'd *have* to go!"

"Maybe I'll try that sometime," Kelly says, and the conversation turns to other things. You feel bad for Kelly, because you know she really wants to exercise. And you feel frustrated with yourself, because you just couldn't find the right way to help her take action.

What went wrong?

In fact, at almost every turn, your efforts were doomed to fail. That's because you were using what I like to call the tell-and-sell approach: you tell someone your reasons for doing something, then try to sell her on them. Unfortunately, no matter how good your reasons or how heartfelt your sales pitch, the tell-and-sell approach almost never works.

What happens when you try to sell someone on your reasons for change? Usually, as in this example, your efforts go nowhere. The other person might agree with you, as Kelly did, but that won't spark a desire to take action. That desire — the motivation to act — lives in each one of us. But the only way to unlock it is with our own reasons.

In the example, you told Kelly to exercise because she would be healthier, live longer, feel better, and have more energy. All good arguments, but they didn't work for Kelly because they weren't *her* reasons. Although she agreed with you, she didn't personalize the reasons or explore how much they meant to her.

You also told Kelly how to take action: hire a trainer. But if she hasn't figured out why she wants to take action, she certainly won't care about how to do so.

Three decades of scientific evidence clearly demonstrate that tell-and-sell methods not only fail to motivate; they also lower the motivation level. That's right. Using the wrong type of encouragement can actually make a person want to do something *less*.

So what works? Here's the secret to Instant Influence: people take action when they hear themselves say *why* they want to. People can tell you all day long that they wish they could do something. But when they tell you why they want to do it, that's when things start to happen. That's Instant Influence in a nutshell. Get someone to tell you why he wants to act, and action is almost sure to follow.

There's a catch, though. Other people can't simply agree with your reasons for change or parrot back to you the reasons they are "supposed" to have. For example: "It's good for my health." "My boss will be happier with me." "It's the right thing to do." They need to dig a little deeper and find their own personal reasons for change, often unexpected reasons that may surprise both of you.

WHAT TO EXPECT FROM INSTANT INFLUENCE

Instant Influence can quickly open someone up to the possibility of change. The actual process of taking action or implementing new behavior may require a bit more time, but this first step is critical.

When you have an Instant Influence conversation with someone, there are four possible outcomes:

1. You have complete success. Your influencee commits to making a change or to taking a step toward positive action. You'll follow up by making an action plan (we'll discuss that in chapter 9) and by continuing to monitor his progress. If necessary, you may want to have a second Instant Influence conversation later on, to revive flagging motivation or to help him further along the path to his next step.

2. You have partial success. Your influencee opens up to change in a way she hasn't before, but she still won't commit to taking action. Give her time to process the conversation in her own way. She may go on to take independent action, or you might need to have another Instant Influence conversation to help her keep moving forward.

3. *You have limited success.* Your conversation ends on a civil note, but it appears to you that very little was accomplished. You've planted a seed that may need time to take root, so remain open to the possibility that more progress was made than you realize. If you don't see any signs of improvement in a week or so, you may want to follow up with another Instant Influence conversation, using some of the suggestions in part II to make the conversation more productive.

4. *You seem to have reached a dead end.* The person refuses to have the conversation or remains highly resistant throughout. As in the previous scenario, be open to the possibility that more progress was made than you realize. If you don't see signs of action in a week, you might want to attempt another Instant Influence conversation, just to keep the door open. Chapter 10 offers tips about how to accept the situation and move on when you feel that you have reached an impasse. Don't give up too quickly, however. People change in their own ways and in their own time. If you're not attentive, you might miss it.

Test Your Instant Influence Skills: Helping People Find Their Own Reasons

Throughout the book, I'll give you opportunities to test your Instant Influence skills. But before you learn how to use this approach, maybe you'd like to find out how good you already are at motivating yourself and others to take action. You may have instinctively been using the Instant Influence technique all along — or you may be realizing that, like most of us, you've relied far too much on tell and sell. Here's a quiz to test your motivational skills.

Imagine that a close friend needs to get a mammogram, but she keeps putting it off. There's a history of breast cancer in her family, so you know it's urgent, but she keeps insisting that she's really busy and will take care of it "next month." You believe (correctly) that she's scared and has irrationally concluded that if she never finds out whether she has cancer, she won't get it. You'd like to help her approach the problem in a more realistic and effective way.

Your goal is to get your friend to schedule a mammogram. Check the boxes next to the statements that you think might help you accomplish that.

☐ I don't get it. It's such a simple procedure. How come you don't want to see the doctor?
☐ What do you think is getting in your way?
☐ Every time I've brought this up, we've had a twenty-minute argument. Why haven't you ever just asked me not to mention this topic again?
☐ Look, let's get real. You don't have to make an appointment.
☐ Don't you think you'll feel a lot better when it's all over and you know the results?
☐ Can I ask a really stupid question? Why are you even thinking about getting a mammogram?
☐ Would you like me to come to the doctor with you?
☐ Do you think maybe you're hoping that if you don't go, nothing will be wrong?
☐ Just for the sake of argument, imagine that you've already gone to the appointment. How do you think you'd feel then?

Analysis:

I don't get it. It's such a simple procedure. How come you don't want to see the doctor? Not effective. By asking your friend why she doesn't want to see the doctor, you are encouraging her to rehearse her reasons for *not* doing something. Instead, you want her to focus on her reasons for doing something. The more she realizes why she wants to get a mammogram, the more likely she is to schedule one. Reminding her why she doesn't want to get one may make any obstacle she perceives seem bigger than it already is.

What do you think is getting in your way? Not effective. Again, focusing on obstacles only makes them seem bigger. Like most of us, your friend may be conflicted: she is reluctant to take action but also has a strong desire to do something. If you focus on her resistance, so will she. If you focus on her desire to take action, she may be able to focus on it, too.

Every time I've brought this up, we've had a twenty-minute argument. Why haven't you ever just asked me not to mention this topic again? Effective. The fact that your friend is arguing with you means that some part of her, however small, does — or at least *might* — want to make an appointment. Otherwise, she'd either change the subject or firmly tell you to stop bringing it up. If someone suggested that you get trained as a rodeo clown, move to Antarctica for six months, or wire your life savings to some investment website you've never heard of, would you argue with him? But if someone suggested a company job-development plan, a vacation in an unexpected place, or a meeting with his financial adviser, you might at least discuss the idea, if only to explain why you don't want to do it. Asking your friend why she's arguing about the mammogram might be useful: it could help her tap into that part of herself that is open, even a little bit, to the idea of having the test.

Look, let's get real. You don't have to make an appointment. Effective. As I did with the GE executives, reminding people that you are talking about *their* choice, not yours, is extremely helpful. As we'll see later in this chapter, we're all subject to the law of psychological reactance, our tendency to resist being told what to do. In fact, when someone tells us that we have to do something, it may set us up for a virtually irresistible compulsion to do the exact opposite. If we want to take action, it really helps to see it as our own choice, not a necessity. While you might worry about this approach backfiring, you don't have to: If the other person really doesn't want to do something, she won't, no matter what you say. But if even a small part of her wants to take action, this approach will free her to find her own reasons for doing so.

Don't you think you'll feel a lot better when it's all over and you know the results? Not effective. You are telling your friend how you think she'll feel when the mammogram is over, and you may or may not be right. But by giving her your take on the situation, you're depriving her of the chance to come up with her own. Helping her imagine the future might actually be helpful (that's the basis for Step 4 of the Instant Influence technique), but only if your friend's vision of the future is truly her own.

Can I ask a really stupid question? Why are you even thinking about getting a mammogram? Effective. Now you're asking your friend to tap into her reasons for doing what you would like her to do. If she discovers her own reasons for making an appointment, she'll make one. If she knows only your reasons, she's likely to keep resisting, even if she agrees with everything you say. This kind of question—Why are you even thinking about this? or, Why *might* you consider it?—is another version of Step 1 of the Instant Influence process. It's a good way to fan even the tiniest spark of possibility ("Maybe I *might* do it") into a glowing flame ("You know, I believe I *will* do it!").

Would you like me to come to the doctor with you? Not effective. This generous offer might be helpful later, but it isn't now. That's because your friend hasn't yet committed to making an appointment. If your friend had said, "I know I'd feel a million times better if I just got it over with, but I can't stand the thought of going there alone," then this would be a wonderful way of offering your support. But until your friend has figured out the why, focusing on the how won't help.

Do you think maybe you're hoping that if you don't go, nothing will be wrong? Not effective. As with the first two examples, this question focuses on the why not rather than the why. Even if you're right about this point, your friend may not be ready to admit it. And if she does agree, knowing why she's scared won't necessarily free her from her fear. She doesn't need more insight into why she doesn't want to make the appointment. She needs more insight into why she *does*.

Just for the sake of argument, imagine that you've already gone to the appointment. How do you think you'd feel then? Effective. Helping your friend visualize what good might come of her action is very useful, because, again, it allows her to tap into her own reasons for making a change. (This is an effective version of Step 4 of Instant Influence.) If imagining that happy day when the appointment is already behind her brings your friend a feeling of relief, then a desire to keep feeling that relief may move her to make the call.

Score:
For every "effective" answer you chose, give yourself 1 point. For every "not effective" answer you chose, subtract 1 point.

4 points: Congratulations! You have a real knack for creating Instant Influence and are probably already quite effective at influencing others. If you'd like to develop your abilities further and learn how to apply them in more situations, even some you once thought impossible, keep reading.

1–4 points: You instinctively understand the kinds of questions that get things moving in the right direction, but you're still missing some opportunities that could make you even more effective. *Instant Influence* can help you fine-tune your instincts and improve your approach.

0 points: Your good instincts and your less effective statements are canceling each other out. Reading *Instant Influence* can help you recognize the kinds of questions that are genuinely effective at producing action and steer you away from questions and statements that only get in the way.

Negative score: You'd like to help but don't yet know how to do so effectively. Don't worry. Once you've mastered the principles in *Instant Influence,* you'll find it much easier to move people to action, and you'll also discover new ways to motivate yourself.

THREE GUIDING PRINCIPLES

Instant Influence is based on three principles:

1. No one absolutely has to do anything; the choice is always yours.
2. Everyone already has enough motivation.
3. Focusing on any tiny bit of motivation works much better than asking about resistance.

These principles derive from the work of such pioneering social psychologists as Jack and Sharon Brehm, Martin Seligman, Leon Festinger, and Daryl Bem,[1] researchers whose theories have been confirmed by literally thousands of studies. So let's take a closer look at the science of Instant Influence.

The Law of Psychological Reactance

The first principle — "No one absolutely has to do anything; the choice is always yours" — is a response to the law of psychological reactance: if someone tells you to do something, you probably won't feel like doing it, even if you might otherwise have wanted to.[2] Widely studied by Jack and Sharon Brehm since 1966, this law has long been the bane of managers, health-care professionals, and parents. In fact, the harder the other person tries to get you to do something — the more he yells at you, insists, threatens you with dire consequences — the less you're going to want to do it, and the less likely you are to actually do it.

Ever since the Brehms identified this key aspect of the human personality, they and other researchers have conducted thousands of experiments, first to investigate whether the Brehms' initial insight was accurate and then to understand this response in more detail.[3] Obviously, there's not room here to review the massive amount of research carried out on this topic, but let me share with you some of the most interesting studies.[4]

In an experiment that has since become famous, researchers invited college students to survey a number of group problem-solving tasks and to rate them high, low, or neutral interest.[5] They were then given time to engage in any task they wanted during two sessions separated by a short break, as experimenters monitored their preferences. However, during the break, "confederates" — student-researchers pretending to be participants — strongly encouraged the subjects to pick certain tasks and to avoid others as they entered the second round.

You've probably guessed what happened next. The tasks the subjects were encouraged to avoid became the very ones that interested them most. In fact, based on their actions, they were even more interested in these "forbidden" items than in the ones they had previously rated "high interest."

Now, at this point you may be thinking, *Sure, forbidden*

fruit is sweetest. Of course the students wanted to do what they were told not to do! But what if the students had been interested in certain tasks and were then instructed to do them? Would they avoid these simply because they had been told to choose them?

In fact, that's exactly what happened. This study, along with numerous follow-ups, showed that people were likely to avoid what they had been told to choose and to choose what they had been told to avoid. This was true even if they had previously shown interest in something. Telling people to choose an activity—even one they liked—almost guaranteed that they would then avoid it. That's how much people dislike being told what to do.

Once the law of psychological reactance was well established among scientists, researchers went on to look at it in more detail. Were there some types of messages, for example, that might have an effect opposite the one intended? In 2005, social scientists James Price Dillard of Pennsylvania State University and Lijiang Shen of the University of Wisconsin at Madison conducted an experiment with 202 UW Madison students.[6] They divided the students into two groups and gave each a different message about the benefits of regular flossing. Although the two messages offered identical information, each was worded differently.

One group was asked to read what was deemed a "low-threat" message focusing on the students' autonomy and right to decide for themselves:

> ... [M]ost people would agree that flossing is worthy of serious consideration.... [G]um disease can lead to other severe problems: heart disease, stroke, diabetes, pneumonia, [which] means that you might want to think about making flossing a regular habit.
>
> If you floss already, keep up the good work. And if you haven't, now might be a good time to start. In fact,

you may want to try it today. It's easy, why not give it a try? Set a goal to floss every day for the next week, starting today.

The second group of students was given a "high-threat" message that stressed the *have to* rather than the *want to*.

> ...Any sensible person can see that there is really no choice when it comes to flossing. You simply have to do it....And the fact that gum disease can become the basis for other severe problems such as stroke and pneumonia makes it just stupid not to floss every single day of your life. So if you floss already, don't stop even for a day. And if you haven't been flossing, right now is the time to start: today.
> Do it because you have to. Floss every single day.... Set a goal for yourself to floss every day for the next week, starting today.

As you might have guessed, students who heard the low-threat message were significantly more likely to floss than were the students who heard the high-threat message. I find this astonishing. Shouldn't a rational person respond to the content rather than the threat level of the message? After all, everyone agrees that flossing is a good idea, and learning about consequences as dire as pneumonia and stroke should strike fear into the heart of even the most careless person. But in fact, the effective message was the one that stressed the students' autonomy, not the consequences of not flossing. More important than avoiding pneumonia or stroke, apparently, is feeling that we are in charge of our own destinies.

Now think about what that might mean in the workplace. If you're trying to motivate a reluctant employee to stop using his cell phone on company time or to show more initiative in taking on extra projects, you might think that threatening to fire him, fine him, or otherwise punish him would be highly effective—your own workplace version of "you have to." Far more effective, though, is helping an employee discover why he wants to comply with the no-cell-phone rule or to expand his workload. Surprising as it may be, respecting your employee's autonomy and leaving the final choice up to him—when coupled with the Instant Influence approach—is likely to be the most effective strategy. The same principle goes for parenting. Counterintuitive as it might seem, our kids respond far better when they know they don't have to do something.

Often, I've noticed, we try to influence others by telling them all the terrible things that will happen if they don't do what we want them to do: "You have to take on more responsibility around here, or I may need to let you go." "You have to lose weight—you're setting yourself up for diabetes." "You'd better get your grades up, or you'll never get into a good college." Most of us have tried this type of scare tactic at least once in our lives, and we've usually met with frustration.

As the high- and low-threat-message experiment makes clear, most people don't respond well to threats. Sometimes they'll argue with you outright: "You can't fire me when Joe is doing even less work—*and* he comes in late all the time!" "My grandfather ate worse than I do, and he lived to be ninety-two!" "I can so get into a good college!" Sometimes they'll tell you they don't care: "Well, go ahead and fire me, then!" "Hey, when your time comes, it comes." "I don't want to go to college anyway."

The law of psychological reactance is hard to disobey. Luckily, there's an easy solution, whether we're trying to motivate others or ourselves. Avoid the have-tos and the threats, and focus on the want-tos and whys that create Instant Influence. Sure, sometimes you might need to impose consequences. But don't use consequences to try to influence someone; other types of motivation work better.

Accessing Our Own Motivation

The second principle of Instant Influence is "Everyone already has enough motivation." It's based in part on research on depression conducted by clinical psychologist Martin Seligman in 2005.[7] One of the most debilitating aspects of depression is the lack of energy and the sense of hopelessness that seem to short-circuit any behavioral change before it begins. If you tell a depressed person that he'll feel better once he gets out and does something fun, he'll likely tell you that he doesn't have the strength and that it won't help anyway.

Seligman wasn't convinced. Perhaps depressed people did have enough motivation to make positive changes in their lives—maybe they just needed to access it. So he gave 577 mildly depressed people an online questionnaire about what they might like to do if they were not depressed.

The people in this study had all described themselves as inactive and not engaged in the world around them. They saw themselves as lacking the energy or motivation to get out and enjoy themselves, and they felt sad and frustrated about their shortcomings. Seligman asked them to keep a daily log for a week—not about what they did or even about what they planned to do, but simply about what they *would* do if they had more energy.

Notice that Seligman had set up a situation in which his subjects couldn't focus on the how ("How can I enjoy myself when I'm so tired?"). That might have gotten people thinking of all the reasons they couldn't take action. Instead, he tried to access motivation by asking people to focus on what they might want. (As you'll see in chapter 3, *might* is one of the most useful words in the Instant Influence vocabulary.)

Amazingly, simply by noticing what they potentially might like to do, these depressed individuals discovered that they were motivated after all. After just one week of thinking about their

30

potential desires, they reported being more active in the world. They also said they felt happier and less depressed.

Resolving Cognitive Dissonance

The third principle of Instant Influence is "Focusing on any tiny bit of motivation works much better than asking about resistance." This is inspired by the work of social psychologist Leon Festinger, who in 1957 explored the notion of cognitive dissonance. Festinger realized that we often have two clashing, or dissonant, ideas about who we are.[8] We believe, for example, that we are depressed and unmotivated, but then we hear ourselves saying, "If I weren't depressed, I'd love to go to the movies," or "If I had the energy, I'd like to meet my friend Sarah for coffee." How can we rectify this dissonance between our statements about ourselves and our behavior? One way is to go out and have fun. Then our actions and our statements about ourselves match. Hearing ourselves say what we want to do helps us find the motivation to do it.

Most of my trainees and coaches greet this insight with skepticism. They can't quite believe that simply saying "I'd really like to do X" will actually make it more likely that the person will, in fact, do X. I assure you that dozens of well-respected studies have verified this point, magical as it may sound. The reason we're so surprised, I think, is because we're used to hearing people say "I *should* do X," and that, of course, has virtually the opposite effect. The more we think we should do something, the *less* likely we may be to do it, particularly when the law of psychological reactance kicks in. That's why Instant Influence is so powerful. It helps people identify their reasons for wanting to do something, and, with that, positive action is almost sure to follow.

In other words, as both Seligman and Festinger discovered, we seem to have a strong desire to align our statements about ourselves with our actions. We grow very uncomfortable if we feel that we don't know ourselves as well as we thought we did. And so we'll take all sorts of extraordinary steps just to prove that we really do know who we are.

You can see how this need for consistency might help us use Instant Influence successfully. Once a person makes even a tentative statement about what she wants, such as, "I might want to be on time for work someday," she's set up a cognitive dissonance that she can't resolve until she's actually on time. Until her actions match her statements, she can't count on herself to know who she is.

For most of us, it's painful and upsetting to find holes in our self-image. The only way to resolve the discomfort is to fulfill our own idea of ourselves. Therefore, if we can get a person to express even the tiniest desire to take action, at least part of her will want to align her behavior with her statements.

Keep in mind that this works only with wants, not with oughts or shoulds or supposed-tos. "I'm supposed to be at work at 9 a.m., but I'm always late" isn't cognitive dissonance. You see yourself as a disobedient person who comes to work late, and you do come to work late. You may not like who you are, but you know who you are. However, if you say to yourself, "I want to get to work on time," and especially if you say why you want to ("I'd be less stressed"; "I could stop feeling guilty about my coworkers covering for me"; "I'd be able to drink the coffee while it's still fresh"), then your behavior is far more likely to catch up with your statement. You must *really* want to get to work on time because you've just given all these reasons why you want to, and so now you do. You breathe a sigh of relief, and the cognitive dissonance disappears.

Putting Behavior First

It probably won't surprise you to learn that not everyone agrees with the theory of cognitive dissonance. In fact, some social scientists, like Daryl Bem, think it's the other way around.[9] Instead of starting with attitudes ("I want to be on time") and moving to behavior ("Look, I just *was* on time"), Bem thinks that behavior is the key ("Hey, I was on time yesterday") and that our attitudes catch up later ("That must mean I like being punctual. Since I like it so much, maybe I'll just keep doing it").

Bem's approach also feeds into Instant Influence. If you can get someone to engage in a behavior—even a tiny baby step— you've got something to build on. Once a person recognizes that he has done something (come to work on time, started running every morning before work, made more healthful food choices), you can help him find the motivation to keep doing it.

Instant Influence often starts with tiny steps. As you saw in the introduction, I didn't try to get the GE executives to commit to my approach. I just asked them to agree to listen to it. I figured that once they agreed to listen, they might be willing to learn and even embrace the program. If your friend is reluctant to schedule a mammogram, forget the mammogram itself; ask her why she might want to look up the doctor's number and write it down. She may think the question sounds odd, but encourage her to answer it anyway. Perhaps she'll say, "Well, if I ever do want to call, I guess looking up the number now will make it easier," or "At least I'll have the information if I need it." Meanwhile, if she does become motivated to write down the number, that one little action makes a big statement: "I am someone who is considering having a mammogram." And someone who is considering having a mammogram might actually go ahead and have one.

Likewise, if you're having a hard time looking for a job, don't start by trying to schedule five interviews. Choose a much smaller step, such as spending ten minutes browsing an online job site. (We'll talk more about defining an appropriate first step in chapter 3.) Making even the tiniest start toward a goal often helps us discover huge reserves of motivation for sticking with it and moving forward.

You can modify Step 1 of the Instant Influence technique to focus on actual behavior. Instead of asking, "Why might you change?" you could ask, "Why have you already taken [some action that represents a tiny step toward changing]?" Or, as I asked the GE executives, "Why did you even agree to show up for this meeting? Why didn't you blow it off like Frank did?" In other words, "Since you are here at the meeting, you must want to be here, so *why* do you want to be here?"

Similarly, you might ask your friend, "Why do you keep arguing about whether you should have a mammogram? Why haven't you ever just asked me not to mention this topic again?" In other words, "Since we're arguing about the mammogram, you must be considering having one, so *why* are you considering having one?" If you're having trouble looking for a job, you might ask yourself, "Why am I even thinking about getting a new job? Why haven't I forgotten all about it?" People's actions often show that they have far more motivation than they are aware of. We can use the evidence of those actions to help them find even more motivation.

Talking about even the slightest hint of motivation works much better than asking about resistance. With all due respect to the scientists involved in the cognitive dissonance dispute, I personally think that sometimes attitude comes first; other times, behavior. Instant Influence draws on both approaches, thereby giving it the greatest chance of success.

A PROVEN APPROACH

Instant Influence isn't just based on well-tested science. It has proven itself in various private and professional settings as well.

- Psychiatric patients
Before: Psychiatric patients hospitalized at St. Barnabas and Union Hospitals in the Bronx, New York, were routinely told

in a very high-threat manner that they absolutely had to follow up with aftercare and other treatment recommendations or else they would get even sicker and would have to reenter the hospital. That high-threat approach produced a compliance rate of only 13 percent, and many patients came back to the hospital repeatedly.

After: After a single one-hour session of Instant Influence conducted for psychiatric patients by undergraduates, compliance rates increased by 250 percent and continued to improve from there as both hospitals made Instant Influence a standard part of patient care. For a while, the hospitals actually stopped using the approach, because too few patients were returning and they were losing money. Since 1994, however, the program has been going strong.[10]

• Probationers and parolees

Before: Probationers and parolees are notorious for not complying with their court-ordered requirements for staying out of jail. Some people even say they'd rather go to jail than have to deal with parole/probation officers, who typically present requirements in a very high-threat way. For example, "If you don't do what I say, you're going to prison." The alternative— leniency—is no better; probationers and parolees often break the terms of their sentence and go directly to jail.

After: Since Connecticut began using Instant Influence in its probation and parole system, return rates have dropped significantly, prison populations are down, and probation officers are reporting increased job satisfaction. Department chiefs are even using Instant Influence to improve their own performance as well as that of their staff: managers and employees are now more punctual, take fewer sick days, turn reports in on time, are better prepared, and tend to volunteer more for special assignments.

• Managers and human resources staff

Before: Just about every manager I train has stories of

frustration. How can he manage the resistant person who cuts him short, has an answer for everything, or does the bare minimum to avoid being fired?

After: After every Instant Influence training session, I get several e-mails saying that it has made a world of difference. They especially love seeing that look in an employee's eye just before she announces her reasons for doing what the manager has spent weeks unsuccessfully trying to get her to do.

- My own coaching clients, consulting clients, and patients

Before: Even I didn't know what to say to people when they told me no. I wanted to help them change, but if they were resistant, I didn't know how to help them progress.

After: All of my Instant Influence clients and patients have made significant progress, even if some of them still have more work to do. I'm far more effective as a coach, consultant, and therapist now that I understand that change must come from within.

REASONS PEOPLE GIVE FOR NOT USING THIS TECHNIQUE

Sometimes, no matter how many statistics and personal examples I cite, trainees, colleagues, or coaching clients object to the idea of Instant Influence. They believe it won't work, or they may have some philosophical or practical difficulties with the approach. Here are some common objections and my responses to them.

- *"Confrontation is necessary."* Yes, sometimes it is. In a dire situation—an intoxicated person trying to drive, an employee making a decision that could cost the company money or you your job—you may need to use physical, social, or economic force. You just don't have time to let the other person find her own reasons. Confrontation also may be necessary on emotional grounds. Sometimes it's less important to get someone to change her behavior than to tell her how you feel. Although it's hard to motivate someone while also expressing your feelings, you may need the emotional honesty or satisfaction that comes from a direct confrontation.

In either case, confrontation won't work forever. In the long term, when the danger is less immediate, your best bet is Instant Influence.

• *"This is manipulative."* It can be. If your influencee is vulnerable or confused, you may be able to convince him that he really does want what you want.

But the goal of Instant Influence is not to manipulate people. It's to help them tap into their own potential reasons for taking a particular action. If you're honest about what you want, then all the cards are on the table. That isn't being manipulative; it's giving someone a chance to discover choices they didn't know they had or wanted.

• *"I don't want to be the other person's therapist."* You shouldn't be. If you think someone really needs a therapist, don't try to meet that need by using this process. You might, however, use the process to motivate the other person to seek professional help.

• *"I won't have enough time with the other person, just one or two minutes."* Ideally, you'll allow at least seven minutes for this process. But sometimes one or two minutes is enough. I've known people who have turned a major corner in their lives by being asked just one of the Instant Influence questions. Asking brief but effective questions that move the other person even a little is better than being ineffective or doing nothing. At least you've given them something to think about!

• *"Other ways work better."* Sometimes, sure, that's true. For some people, incentives, rewards, or punishments might be more effective motivators than this particular technique. And for some people, a combination of this technique and external rewards or punishments is most effective. If the other approaches you're using aren't working to your satisfaction, though, Instant Influence may help.

• *"Why should I even have to do this?"* Often, people feel frustrated by how long they've been trying to get someone to change. The idea of learning a whole new approach can be daunting, annoying, or simply discouraging.

If you're ready to write someone off, you can forget about Instant Influence and simply terminate the relationship. But if that's not an option, or not the option you choose, then putting in a little more effort by using a proven, effective technique might make a difference. If you try this method and it doesn't work, at least you know that you did the best you could.

• *"It won't work, and I'll be worse off than before."* In most cases, this approach *does* work. But if it doesn't, the only way you're "worse off" is that now you have a clearer picture of your situation. You now may be more ready to accept that your difficult employee, your unreasonable boss, or your stubborn partner really isn't going to behave the way you'd like him to. Once you've given it your best shot, you can move on to accepting your situation and figuring out what you'd like to do next. (We'll look at acceptance in chapter 10.)

I hope what you've learned in this chapter has persuaded you to give Instant Influence a try. Let's continue to chapter 2, which will show you how to reinforce autonomy, the best possible preparation for an Instant Influence conversation.

CHAPTER TWO

Reinforcing Autonomy

T he six steps of Instant Influence are the heart of the process. But those steps will be far more effective if you prepare for them by reinforcing the other person's autonomy. Autonomy is the basis of the first two Instant Influence principles:

1. No one absolutely has to do anything; the choice is always yours.
2. Everyone already has enough motivation.

In other words, people will do what they want to do. We don't need to force them, just let them find their own reasons to do something. In fact, if we do try to force them, the law of psychological reactance will probably cause them to resist.

When we allow people to find their own reasons, they can agree to change in a surprisingly short time. Why? Because each of us carries our motivation within. Every reluctant employee who shows up for an evaluation, every HR manager who argues against a new procedure, every prospective

customer, every skeptical potential client who comes to a negotiating session, is already motivated on some level — to work
out the problem, find the best procedure, or enter into a productive relationship. Reinforcing an influencee's autonomy
("This decision is really up to you"; "I have my own ideas but
the final choice is yours") makes it that much easier for him to
find his own reasons.

You can also reinforce your own autonomy. Suppose you're
trying to start a new exercise plan. Remind yourself that you
don't actually have to start on Monday. You could put it off a
week, two weeks, maybe even forever. After all, you don't absolutely have to do anything. Once you understand that you don't
have to exercise, you can go on to ask yourself *why* you might
want to.

It can require a huge leap of faith to tell an employee, a
coachee, a child, a romantic partner, or a patient that the next
move really is up to her — that this is her decision. Most of the
time, we want to scream, "You idiot! Don't you know what's
going to happen to you if you don't quit smoking!" or "The
next time you pull something like that, I'm out of here!" or
"How can you jeopardize your entire future by not doing your
homework?" Again, I'm not suggesting that there shouldn't be
consequences. But remember that people won't act for your
reasons — only for their own. Reinforcing their autonomy is
the best way to prepare them for Instant Influence.

Does this sound hard to believe? That's not surprising. Most
of the people I train are skeptical, too. When you put Instant
Influence into practice, which you'll be ready to do at the end
of chapter 3, you'll see for yourself just how well it can work.
Meanwhile, let's take a closer look at the two key principles of
reinforcing autonomy.

NO ONE ABSOLUTELY HAS TO DO ANYTHING;
THE CHOICE IS ALWAYS YOURS

This principle stems from the law of psychological reactance. As you'll recall, that law has been validated in thousands of studies showing that people dislike being told what to do. You could almost say that the fastest way to get people to do something is to tell them *not* to do it. (I always think of Mark Twain's hero Tom Sawyer, who made out like a bandit by refusing to let the neighbor-boys help him whitewash his fence—when they begged him to let them do it, he accepted their most prized possessions in exchange.)

This principle is based on four assumptions:

1. Each of us is free to choose the behaviors in which we want to engage.

2. Other people can threaten that freedom with certain types of statements, such as "You have to do this" or "You can't do that."

3. We tend to react very negatively when our freedom is verbally threatened: arguing, feeling angry or discouraged, justifying the behavior that was criticized, and/or renewing our intention to continue it.

4. Our threatened freedom can be restored by such autonomy-enhancing statements as "It's up to you," "You're the only one who can decide to do this," and "This is really your decision." If we're motivating ourselves, we should remember that we don't absolutely have to do anything. If we're motivating someone else, we should remind him that he doesn't absolutely have to do anything, and then assure him that we accept and support his autonomy.

It can be difficult to remember that "no one absolutely has to do anything," especially in situations where we feel responsible—

for another person's well-being or for a large project we're directing, for example. But even if there are times when we don't like acknowledging another person's freedom to do or to not do something, accepting this freedom is key.

EVERYONE ALREADY HAS ENOUGH MOTIVATION

Although I didn't realize it when I first developed Instant Influence, the idea that everyone already has enough motivation is gaining popularity in the business world. For example, General Electric sees this notion as highly compatible with their "organic growth" philosophy, the idea that a business should grow organically and from within. Just as businesses shouldn't be forced to grow, neither should people be forced to change — they, too, can change organically and from within. The folks at GE began calling this the "green principle" of Instant Influence. Some execs even started talking about "sustainable motivation."

What I like about these images is that they allow us to visualize small amounts of motivation as well as large ones. In an era of such positive thinking advocates as Tony Robbins and Napoleon Hill, we might believe that the only effective motivation is the powerhouse, the raging fire, the unstoppable juggernaut — a degree of motivation that most people simply don't have.

Of course, some people do possess extraordinary levels of motivation — as we learned in the introduction, my father is one — but even they might not always feel motivated. Although my father trekked across Europe and built a new life in America, he had trouble accessing the motivation to quit smoking, as I'll explain in chapter 6. And when he did begin to quit smoking, he started small: just two fewer cigarettes each week. You may need a powerhouse to give up smoking cold turkey, but who can't manage a change so small you might almost miss it? More often than not, we're looking at tiny amounts of motivation, minuscule sparks rather than giant fires.

And yet, to get the job done, that little spark may be all you need. That's because, as the Chinese proverb has it, a journey of a thousand miles begins with a single step. While most of us have difficulty imagining the journey's end, virtually all of us can find the motivation to make a small beginning. And that step can lead to another, then another, and another. Then, before we know it, we're there.

This isn't just an optimistic statement. Numerous studies have shown that people having any level of motivation are capable of making dramatic changes. When people have rated their motivation on a scale of 1 to 10, for example, you might think that the 10s would be more likely to take action than the 2s. Not so! In fact, several of my own studies found that people who made significant changes in their behavior appeared all along the motivational continuum, not just at the high end.[1]

Studies have also shown that people are more likely to be motivated by their own wishes and desires than by anything imposed from the outside. Whether we're talking about threats, promises, financial rewards, or honors, these extrinsic factors don't hold a candle to motivation that's been mobilized from within.[2]

Although for years motivational experts have tried to come up with a questionnaire to predict future performance, no one has yet been able to do it.[3] Why? Because motivation is a completely individual matter. Your motivation is within you, and only you can fully access it. No matter how cleverly I question you or how complicated a survey I prepare, I won't be able to figure out what is finally going to get you moving. Only one person knows how to truly ignite your inner spark, and that person is you.

THE IMPORTANCE OF RESTORING AUTONOMY

Restoring someone's autonomy is crucial if the Instant Influence process is going to work. It doesn't matter whether that autonomy was threatened by you or by previous authority figures. Your job is to establish, in no uncertain terms, that "no one absolutely has to do anything." Even if the alternative is highly unpleasant — job loss, illness, or death — we almost always have a choice.

Occasionally, you may meet a manager, probation officer, teacher, or parent who rules by force. If someone under their supervision doesn't do what they want, these dictators enforce swift and merciless punishments. They yell, they fine, they threaten; they might even resort to physical violence. And, for a short while, that approach may work.

In the long run, though, their power loses its effect. The child rebels or withdraws. The student flunks or drops out or moves on to the next class. The probationer goes to jail. And the employee quits, transfers, or learns to do the least amount of work needed to get by.

If you are trying to help a victim of this type of treatment — or if you're trying to make up for your own previous authoritarian behavior — you may need to spend some extra time reinforcing your influencee's autonomy. I once worked with a supervisor who was frustrated by the new guy who had transferred into her department. He seemed like a real "screwup," to use her words, "easily the laziest, least motivated person" she'd ever worked with. He came in late, he missed every deadline, he took two-hour lunches, and he made dozens of careless mistakes. If you wanted a poster child for lack of motivation, this guy was it.

When she checked with his previous department, however, she was baffled. He'd always had a perfect record, and his former supervisor had given him high marks for everything. Between his department and hers, what had gone wrong?

It turned out that this former supervisor was an office dictator who made life so stressful for his employees that the turnover rate in his department was the highest in the company. Under that supervisor, the employee did indeed perform "perfectly," but he also transferred out of the department as soon as he was allowed to. Still traumatized by that reign of terror, he had lost all motivation for doing his job well.

Through Instant Influence, his new supervisor was able to reinforce his autonomy and engage his motivation. It took a little time, but eventually she got through to him. He started performing at an even higher level than he had in his old department, and he also became one of her most loyal, devoted colleagues. "I doubted you for a while," she told me in an e-mail, "but I'm glad you were right: nothing compares to motivation from within."

Many of the managers, doctors, and teachers I've trained find it frustrating to learn that they need to reestablish someone's autonomy. "I never told that guy he had to do anything," a manager might say. "Why do I have to take all my time to make him feel better?" "I always give my students room to choose," a teacher might complain. "Why should I have to keep proving that I'm not like other teachers?"

It doesn't matter. Even if you have never threatened your influencee's freedom, someone else most certainly has. Nor does it matter in which domain a person's freedom has been threatened. The doctor who told him that he had to quit smoking, the girlfriend who told him that he had to dress better, and the teacher who told him that he had to do his homework have all taken their toll on your resistant influencee. From his point of view, people have been telling him what to do all his life, and he's sick and tired of it. Now you are just one more autonomy-threatening voice, and he's going to tune you out, too. You must restore his autonomy to open the lines of communication. And if there have been several authority figures undermining his autonomy, you must take into account the cumulative effect of all those threats and work to counter it.

How to Restore Someone's Autonomy

So how do you restore someone's autonomy? Fortunately, it's easy.

1. Come out with the strongest autonomy-reinforcing statement that you can honestly make. If you're dealing with a loved one, a client, or a business partner, you may be able to stress complete autonomy:

> "This is your choice, not mine."
> "It's completely your decision."
> "You're free to do whatever you want."
> "I can't make this choice for you — it's up to you."

If you're a parent, an employer, a supervisor, or someone else responsible for imposing consequences, you may need to word things slightly differently, leaving room for the fact that the other person is operating within certain constraints:

> "What you decide at this point is up to you."
> "Right now I'm not interested in my reasons but in *your* reasons."
> "Even though others will have their own reactions, you're the only one who can make this decision."
> "Only you can decide what you want to do. Of course, your choice will have consequences. But it's still your choice to make — and your consequences to choose."

Some managers, parents, and other authority figures find this to be such a switch from their usual approach that they're at a bit of a loss at first. If you'd like to try it but feel somewhat anxious, prepare one or two autonomy-reinforcing statements ahead of time. Soon you'll find that reinforcing someone's autonomy has become second nature.

2. If a situation is difficult or unfair, say so, but always return responsibility to the influencee. The influencee may insist that something isn't easy or fair or consistent. If you agree, say so. If you don't, at least acknowledge the influencee's point of view ("I understand this doesn't seem fair to you"). Always respect her right to see things her way, while insisting that she take responsibility for her actions.

I once worked with a manager who had to enforce a rule one of her employees objected to. The employee had filed a grievance, but the matter had not yet been settled. Remembering what I'd taught her about autonomy-enhancing statements, the supervisor said, "I understand that you're fighting that rule, and I can see why it might seem unfair. But the rule is still on the books, and your grievance hasn't yet been heard. What is your plan in the meantime?" Note that instead of telling the employee what to do, she reinforced his autonomy by asking him what he intended to do.

"Well," replied the employee, "I don't think I should have to follow this rule while I'm fighting it."

Before learning about Instant Influence, the supervisor would have gotten locked into a power struggle, insisting that the employee had to follow the rule. Instead she said, "I can see your point, and I'd like to stress that you never *have* to follow this or any other rule — there's always a choice. But what might be in it for you if you did follow the rule, just in the short run?"

The employee thought for a minute. "I might have more credibility at the hearing if they see that I've been following the rule anyway." By being allowed to choose what he wanted to do, the employee talked himself into following the rule even as he planned to fight it, the supervisor avoided a power struggle, and good relations were preserved. "If I'd insisted that he follow the rule, I know he would have balked," she told me afterward. "But by respecting his autonomy, I left him room to make a decision that worked for all of us."

3. Be honest about what you want. Nobody likes to be manipulated. One way to make sure that you're not manipulating people you are trying to motivate is to acknowledge your agenda:

> I'd like to see you come to work on time. Frankly, it's making us both look bad that you've been late at least twice a week for the past month. We've spoken about this before, and I know it hasn't gone well. I've tried to get you to do things my way—and, of course, I have my own supervisor to answer to—but in the end, whether or not you come to work on time is up to you. So I'd really like to hear from you about this. *Why might you want to get to work on time for the next five business days? What would be in it for you?*

The italicized words are Step 1 of the Instant Influence process (i.e., Why might you change?), but the sentences that come before it are the autonomy-reinforcing preparation. Notice that nothing in what you've said commits you to anything. You aren't agreeing that the employee can come in whenever he wants, nor are you offering to protect him from the wrath of your supervisor. But by making it clear that this is his decision, you've obeyed the law of psychological reactance, giving him room to find his own reasons to start being punctual.

4. Discuss the consequences in another conversation or at the end of this one. Whether you're dealing with an employee, a loved one, a child, or a stranger, you might find it frustrating to focus so much energy on the other person's autonomy. "What about what *I* want?" you might ask. "I can't just let him come to work at any old time!" "Don't I have any say here at all? Does she get to call all the shots in this relationship?" "He's just a kid! Am I supposed to let him have his way whenever he wants?"

In fact, you are free to carry out any consequences within your purview. Depending on the rules of your company, you can fire, fine, or otherwise discipline an employee. In a personal relationship, you can express anger, withdraw emotionally, or even break off the relationship altogether. You can discipline your child.

You may also have a responsibility to warn the person that consequences are coming. "If your grades stay at this level, you may not get into college," a parent might say.

The important point, though, is that ultimately the other person is still free to choose her own actions. Except in very rare circumstances—when you're committing someone to a mental institution, for example, or declaring a person incompetent to gain legal custody—adults really are free to make their own decisions, no matter how self-destructive, dangerous, or just plain stupid those decisions might sometimes seem to be. Even our children, for good or ill, are at least somewhat free to do what they want; we can't watch them every minute. It's in our interest to get out of the way whenever we can and let others face the consequences of their actions. The more they do so, the more motivated they'll be to choose responsibly.

You can support this process by viewing your role as helping someone make the most fully informed decision possible, rather than getting him to choose what you want him to. That's why I suggest saving any discussion of consequences for a separate conversation. Even then, however, it's best not to lead with your own rendition of the consequences. Instead, ask one of the following questions to prompt the person to imagine the consequences for himself:

> "Let's talk through this. If you continue to come late to work, what do you think will happen?"
>
> "I'm curious. With grades like these, what do you think might happen to your plans for college?"
>
> "If you keep making plans for both of us without asking me first, how do you see our relationship going?"

The hope is that the person you're speaking with will recognize the consequences of his actions and then make a genuine choice rather than simply follow the law of psychological reactance. But a genuine choice requires true autonomy.

One of the most interesting fields of psychological research concerns intrinsic and extrinsic motivation: the study of people doing things autonomously and for their own sake versus doing something for a reward. The results are overwhelming: Intrinsic motivation is far more powerful. In fact, occasionally when you start rewarding behavior that people were already doing, they start doing it *less*.[4]

Psychologist Edward L. Deci conducted a study in which twenty-four undergraduate psychology students were asked to come in for three days to work on a problem involving a puzzle.[5] In theory, the puzzle was intrinsically motivating because its pieces could be put together in many different ways, allowing students to keep finding new solutions. And indeed, the students all told the researchers that they found the puzzle interesting and fun, some even choosing to work on it during the eight-minute break in the middle of their session.

On the second day, half the students were given an external reward: They were paid a dollar for each of four puzzle solutions that they completed within a specified time, and they were allowed to keep trying to find still more unpaid solutions. The other half of the students received no money.

You've probably already guessed what happened next. On the second day, the students who were being paid chose to spend far less of their free time working on the puzzle than they had the first day. Even on the third day, when those students were no longer paid, they never returned to their original activity levels. Meanwhile, the students who had never been paid in the first place kept spending more and more free time on the puzzle.

A great deal of business research has come to similar conclusions. For example, many studies have found that bonuses don't promote more dedicated performance. Instead, they seem to motivate unethical behavior: shortcuts, cheating, and other ways to get the bonus that don't involve doing a good job.[6]

I'm not saying that there are no circumstances in which an extrinsic reward might be helpful — certainly, there are many. But it's very important to keep the balance firmly in favor of *intrinsic* rewards: the satisfaction that comes from doing your job well, for your own reasons. Study after study confirms that internal motivation really is the most reliable way to ensure good performance.

Test Your Instant Influence Skills:
Reinforcing Autonomy

Can you tell the difference between statements that truly promote autonomy and those that only seem to? Check the box next to each statement in the list that genuinely reinforces autonomy. Then read on to find out how you did.

☐ I think it's a good idea, but that's just me.
☐ I thought you were going to take care of this.
☐ I thought you really wanted this.
☐ You're going to have to make a decision.
☐ It's up to you to do what you need to do.

- [ ] You've told me how much you want this.
- [ ] Only a fool would do that.
- [ ] There are pros and cons to both choices; only you can decide how things add up for you.
- [ ] Someone who's really concerned about her health would do this.
- [ ] The only way to get organized is to [insert your recommendation].
- [ ] I don't really see any other way of doing this.
- [ ] Sometimes you just have to bite the bullet and do it.
- [ ] We may not like this rule, but we still have to follow it.
- [ ] I can't understand why you're hesitating — just give it a try.
- [ ] You don't even want to think about what will happen if you don't do it.
- [ ] You know you can do better than that.
- [ ] You have to put your heart in it.
- [ ] You of all people should know better.
- [ ] It's up to you to decide what you want and how to get it.
- [ ] You have to at least give it a try.
- [ ] This is not what I expect from someone like you.
- [ ] I'm sure if you'd try, you could do better.
- [ ] I know you've tried really hard, but I need you to try a little harder.
- [ ] You know you haven't given it your all.
- [ ] I know what *I'd* like you to do.
- [ ] You have a responsibility to this team.
- [ ] You of all people should be behind this.
- [ ] It's up to you to do what needs to be done.
- [ ] You're really going to feel bad if you can't make this happen.
- [ ] If it were completely up to me, here's what I'd like to see happen.
- [ ] Think about the repercussions of what you're doing.
- [ ] It makes me so happy and proud that you've changed.

☐ You decide; you can do it however you want.

☐ I knew that eventually you would see it my way.

☐ I was getting really worried that I wasn't being an effective motivator.

☐ I knew that our last conversation was going to get through to you.

☐ You don't have to do it, but please consider how your actions are affecting the rest of us.

Hint:

There are only six autonomy-reinforcing statements in the list. Most of the others sound as though they're supporting autonomy, but they're really not. How many statements did you pick? Take another look to see if you can identify the supportive six autonomy-reinforcing statements.

Autonomy-reinforcing statements:

I think it's a good idea, but that's just me. Stating an opinion and acknowledging that it is only your opinion gives the other person freedom to have his or her own response.

There are pros and cons to both choices; only you can decide how things add up for you. This statement focuses on both the other person's right to make a decision and the idea that the decision is being left to him.

It's up to you to decide what you want and how to get it. Note that this statement focuses on what the other person wants, not what he needs, has to do, or should do.

I know what I'd *like you to do.* This is another way of saying that you do, indeed, have an opinion. But you're also acknowledging that that opinion is your preference, not necessarily the other person's.

If it were completely up to me, here's what I'd like to see happen. Again, stating your own opinion while acknowledging that it's only your opinion gives the other person room to decide. It's easy to follow this with further support for the other person's autonomy: "But it's not up to me. This is *your* decision."

You decide; you can do it however you want. You can only make this kind of statement if it's true, of course. But if the other person really is free to choose her own way of doing something, this is a terrific way of taking yourself out of the situation and leaving the responsibility with her.

Autonomy-undermining statements:
Before you read through this list, revisit the quiz to see if you can explain what's wrong with each autonomy-sapping statement. Then read below for the responses they might provoke in a resistant listener.

I thought you were going to take care of this. "Wow, you're not giving me much of a choice here. No matter what *I* decide or choose, I have to 'take care of this.'"

I thought you really wanted this. "This makes me feel boxed in. You're telling me what I want, instead of letting me express my own wishes."

You're going to have to make a decision. "You're telling me what I 'have to' do. That doesn't make me feel very autonomous."

It's up to you to do what you need to do. "You're telling me what I 'need' to do. That doesn't make me feel very autonomous."

You've told me how much you want this. "You're using my words against me, but you're not asking me what I want."

Only a fool would do that. "That may be true, but it's a high-threat statement. It gives me no choice but to agree with you. And when I don't have a choice, I feel like rebelling, withdrawing, or, at best, paying lip service. I don't feel like being responsible, cooperative, or productive."

Someone who's really concerned about her health would do this. "Ditto."

The only way to get organized is to [insert your recommendation]. "Ditto."

I don't really see any other way of doing this. "Ditto."

Sometimes you just have to bite the bullet and do it. "Ditto."

We may not like this rule, but we still have to follow it. "You're telling me what I 'have to' do. That undermines my autonomy."

I can't understand why you're hesitating—just give it a try. "I can't feel autonomous when you're giving me a command. A question would be so much better: 'Why might you want to give this a try?' or 'What good might come out of it if you gave this a try?'"

You don't even want to think about what will happen if you don't do it. "This seems like the very essence of a threat."

You know you can do better than that. "Maybe I know that and maybe I don't, but I still haven't been allowed to make my own decision."

You have to get your heart in it. "Telling me I 'have to' do something is more likely to turn me off than to help me 'get my heart in it.'"

You of all people should know better. "This doesn't give me any room to disagree."

You have to at least give it a try. "Again, a question would support my autonomy far more than telling me that I 'have to' do something: 'What might happen if you gave it a try?'"

This is not what I expect from someone like you. "This may make me feel ashamed, but it does not support my autonomy. The issue is not what you expect of me, but what I expect of myself."

I'm sure if you'd try, you could do better. "Maybe I can, but do I want to? You haven't asked me what I want, so you're not supporting my autonomy."

I know you've tried really hard, but I need you to try a little harder. "So now we're talking about what you need? What about what I need?"

You know you haven't given it your all. "You're not asking me what I think or know; you're just telling me. How do you know what I know? How do you know what my 'all' is?"

You have a responsibility to this team. "Maybe so, but it does not promote my autonomy to tell me this. You might ask me about it: 'What kind of relationship do you want with this team?' 'In my view, you have a responsibility to this team, but perhaps that's not how you see it. What's your idea about you and the team?'"

You of all people should be behind this. "You're not asking me what I think; you're telling me what I should think. Now I feel like disagreeing, even if deep down I agree."

It's up to you to do what needs to be done. "But you are saying 'what needs to be done,' which doesn't leave me much autonomy."

You're really going to feel bad if you can't make this happen. "Now you're telling me what I want and how I'm going to feel about it. Not much autonomy there."

Think about the repercussions of what you're doing. "Another command. What if you put this same thought in the form of a question: 'How do you think your behavior is going to affect the rest of the staff?' Or better yet: 'How would you like your behavior to affect the rest of the staff? What kinds of repercussions would you like to cause?'"

It makes me so happy and proud that you've changed. "Oh, so all my changing was to make *you* happy? I thought we were talking about me and my autonomy, not you and your feelings."

I knew that eventually you would see it my way. "But I prefer to think that I'm seeing it my way. Now I'm not sure if I'm really autonomous or if I'm just caving in to you."

I was getting really worried that I wasn't being an effective motivator. "Why is this about you and your motivational skills? I thought it was about me and what I wanted to do."

I knew that our last conversation was going to get through to you. "But I prefer to think that I made my own decision. Now you're telling me that you 'got through to me.' So am I autonomous or just following orders?"

You don't have to do it, but please consider how your actions are affecting the rest of us. "You're giving me a command again. Instead of telling me what to consider, why don't you ask me a question? 'How would you like to affect the rest of us? What effect would you like your actions to have?' That would really reinforce my autonomy!"

WHAT IF THEY DON'T WANT TO DO WHAT YOU'RE ASKING?

That's the question everybody always asks, and no wonder. As we saw in chapter 1, many of us have spent years trying to motivate people by having them rehearse their reasons for not doing something, asking such questions as: "Why don't you want to?" "What's getting in your way?" "Why do you think you're having such a hard time?" In other words, we've had a lot of experience thinking that people really don't want to do what we believe is good for them.

But studies indicate that focusing on resistance only makes people more resistant, whereas reinforcing autonomy and focusing on motivation are likely to have positive results. Research has shown, for example, that people are more likely to undertake health-related behavior — healthy eating, exercise, taking medications as prescribed — if they have heard about the benefit of doing it rather than the downside of not doing it. This is known as *gain framing* or *positive-message framing.*[7]

Gain framing is effective because of those commonsense facts that social scientists are always rediscovering: people don't want to do things that they think will be hard. Changing your behavior in any way — to lose weight, to meet a deadline, or for any other reason—sounds hard. And if you ask people why they aren't doing something, it starts to sound even harder.

What approach can bring about influence? Shifting the conversation away from what's hard to the potential upside: "What might be good about this behavior for you?" "Why might you want to do this?" "If the obstacles were to magically disappear, why might this be something you would choose?"

In my experience, most of us are used to framing things negatively, so it takes a bit of practice to present things differently. But think about it. Why might you want to put a little effort into that kind of reframing? What would be in it for you?

GETTING STARTED

Once my trainees understand the power that comes from reinforcing someone's autonomy, they are usually eager to get started but may be at a loss as to how to go about it. If you are also wondering how to proceed, read through the suggestions that follow and choose the ones that you like best. Then practice with a friend until you're comfortable.

Directly Reinforcing Autonomy

There are lots of ways you can reinforce someone's autonomy. Here are some effective statements that you can use as is or put into your own words to let your influencee know that you are not going to force a change.

- Let's call it like it is. Things haven't been going well between us. We've talked about attendance, deadlines, whatever, and we haven't gotten anywhere. I'm not saying it's you; I'm not saying it's me. Let's try something different.

- I want a win-win here.
- Hard as it might be to believe that someone wants a win-win in this situation, that is my personal goal.
- I know that previous managers have handled things differently [or, I know that in the past I have handled things differently]. But I'm not going to try to make you give in on [this point]. And I don't want to talk about [this point], as much as what [this point] might do for both of us.
- I know that you've come to me time and again saying that this is not a good procedure in the office.
- I know that we've locked horns on this.
- I know doing things this new way has been tough for you.
- I believe this is completely up to you.
- I know that we've had some tension around this.
- I know that you probably don't want to talk about this, and it's hard for me, too.
- I know things have been tense, but my aim today is to address this differently, to have a different conversation...

Asking Permission to Use Instant Influence

You also can show your commitment to another person's autonomy by asking permission to use Instant Influence or at least by acknowledging that you're using it. Mention Instant Influence by name, or ask if you can begin a process that you think might be helpful. My trainees always ask me, "What if I request their permission and they say no?" I promise you—people almost never say no, especially if you've just reinforced their autonomy and are sincerely asking permission for a more productive conversation. If you do get a rare, negative response, ask if you can bring up the topic at a more convenient time and then do. If that doesn't work, read chapter 10 to learn how to accept the situation.

- I'd like your permission to try a new approach here. Will it be all right if I ask you a few questions?
- Let's talk about things in a different way this time, okay?
- If I could ask you a few questions that I really think could help you, would you like to hear them?
- I know that this is going to sound odd, but would you mind if we try talking about this in a new way?
- Clarifying ahead of time what we each want to get out of this would be really good. What do you think?
- I'm going to try something that I learned from a book. I'm not trying to make you a guinea pig, but I really think it will help. It may sound awkward at first, but could you bear with me?

TIPS FOR DELIVERING YOUR MESSAGE

- *It's okay not to be cheerful or positive when you speak to someone. You can be neutral, sad, frustrated, tired, or even pissed off — and so can he.* Just because everyone already has enough motivation doesn't mean they have to be cheerful about it. Some of my biggest leaps forward have come when I've felt angry, discouraged, or frustrated, either with myself or with someone I'm supposed to be motivating. Recognizing cognitive dissonance — the gap between what we say about ourselves and what we actually *do* — often makes people feel frustrated or irritated. Still, those are constructive feelings that might spur us to change.
- *If you feel a negative emotion or if you see that emotion in the other person, consider acknowledging it.* "I know we haven't always gotten along," you might say to a recalcitrant employee. "I don't blame you for feeling frustrated with this situation — I'm frustrated, too." If you're trying to use Instant Influence to persuade a supervisor to let you try out a new project, and she expresses annoyance, you might say, "I know you've got a lot of

work to do and you aren't too happy with me right now, but would you be willing to hear me out anyway?" Or perhaps, "Would you be available to discuss this at a better time?"

• *If it's appropriate, mirror the other person's objection or complaint.* "I get why you hate turning these reports in every Friday—I hate my paperwork, too." "If I were in your position, that's exactly how I'd feel." "I don't blame you—that bothers me, too." You can mirror—that is, repeat or reflect—a concern, even when you don't agree, just to show that you've heard and understood. By actively listening, which is another name for mirroring or reflecting, you make it more likely that the other person will listen to you.

TAKE A BREATH AND COUNT TO FIVE

You've gotten your employee, boss, colleague, or loved one to agree to a conversation. You've made your autonomy-enhancing statement and asked permission to use Instant Influence. Now comes the hard part: *pause.*

That's right. Pause. I want you to count silently to yourself, "One-Mississippi, two-Mississippi, three-Mississippi..." This is tough, because you're going to really want to break the silence if the other person hasn't spoken yet, but keep breathing and keep counting: "four-Mississippi, five-Mississippi."

Okay. If she hasn't said anything by the five-second mark, you can begin the Instant Influence process. But it's extremely useful to give the person you're talking to that uncomfortable period of silence, because she may want to jump in and express some feelings of her own. And since the whole goal of Instant Influence is to allow her to tap into her own reasons for doing whatever you might like her to do, you want her to be an active participant in the conversation right from the beginning.

If during that five-second pause you sense that the other

person wants to talk but needs more encouragement, you can say something neutral like, "I've been giving this a lot of thought" or "I'm sure that between us, we can work this out."

What if the other person gives you attitude? "Yes, it *has* been difficult around here," an employee might say. "That's because you're always giving Carla the great leads, and I get the leftovers. And then when I complain about it, you never listen to me!" At that point, your goal is to echo her opinion, not necessarily that you agree or are happy to hear it — remember, you don't have to be cheerful. And if you're feeling angry or discouraged, it's okay to say so. Your main goal is to establish an open atmosphere in which you have permission to use the six steps. Here are some possible responses, all of which lead right into Step 1 of Instant Influence: Why might you change? Feel free to put Step 1 in your own words (here indicated by sentences in italics).

- Yes, I hear that. That is how it's gone so far. I'd like to do something different if we could. *How might you benefit from following the procedure we're talking about?*
- There are two sides here. Up to now, I've been the only one talking about the other side. I'm trying to find out how you might benefit from that other side. *So, what, if anything, might you get out of doing things this other way?*
- We have looked mainly at the downside of doing it the way we currently are. And I respect that that's your opinion. I'm not going to try to make you change. But I do feel that we haven't given the other side of the argument a fair shake. So, *what would be helpful — not to me but to you — if we were to do it the other way?*

If you meet with further objections, continue answering them with autonomy-reinforcing statements. For example, if your employee (or your friend or teenager) says, "I see what you're doing. You're trying to get me to talk myself into this," here are some possible responses:

- No, only if there's some genuine benefit to you. But since we've never talked about it, how would we know?
- I know this hasn't gone well, and I've heard your objections. The fact remains that I can't make you do this, I wouldn't want to make you do this, and you don't absolutely have to do it. But if you did do it, how might it benefit you?
- In a way, you're right—I would like you to go along with this—but only if you decide that you genuinely want to.

PUT THE RESPONSIBILITY WHERE IT BELONGS

Your main goal is to see better results: at work, at home, with yourself. But when you've used this process with other people, especially at work, there is a nice side benefit: the sense that everyone is taking responsibility for his or her own behavior. All too often, when we're supervising others or even when we're emotionally involved with them, we feel that the weight of the world is on our shoulders and that how they behave is completely up to us. What a relief it is to say, "No, how you behave really is up to you."

As one of my trainees explained: "It's such a relief that I don't have to have all the answers anymore. In some way, I really don't care if they change or not. They're responsible for their jobs, and I'm responsible for mine, and that's the way it should be!"

One final note of caution: Although it's fine for you to conduct these conversations in any mood or emotional state that feels natural and appropriate to the situation, what will *not* work is if you are more invested in winning than in coming up with the best possible solution. A desire to triumph in a power struggle is something that everyone in authority is familiar with. Whether you're a boss confronting an angry employee, a therapist treating a resistant patient, or a parent arguing with a stubborn teenager, sometimes you just want the other person to say, "You're right. I'm wrong, and I'll do exactly what you say." And sometimes that is what happens.

Usually, though, especially with Instant Influence, the other person leaves with new motivation to do something productive, something that you are probably going to benefit from, but he won't necessarily give you credit for it or acknowledge your point of view. In fact, if the process is working really well, whatever decision he makes is going to seem to him like his idea, not yours. He suddenly wants to come in early; he suddenly wants to get his paperwork done on time; he suddenly wants to do his homework before the good TV shows come on — all for his own reasons. He may even be critical of you for not having heard him out before or for withholding this great new solution that he has just discovered: "Wow, I just figured out that if I do my homework as soon as I get home from school, I'll have more time to watch TV later on. If you're so smart, why didn't you ever tell me that?"

Likewise, people sometimes do even more than they have agreed to, just to make it clear that they are in charge. More times than I can count, I've heard about employees who turned in reports ahead of schedule, showed up earlier than expected, or otherwise adjusted their behavior to exceed office standards, instead of falling below them as they did previously. I've seen my own patients commit to sticking to a weight-loss plan for one week and then triumphantly — almost smugly — announce that they've "eaten perfectly" for an entire month. My kids, too, have been known to finish their homework early or clean up their rooms before being reminded, and then they throw it in my face, saying they're *way* more responsible than I ever give them credit for.

When these things happen, I smile and say nothing. But in my mind, I'm silently giving thanks for the power of autonomy.

CHAPTER THREE

The Six Steps to Instant Influence

hen Roger took over as human resources vice president at a midsized manufacturing firm, he inherited an office full of discontent, demoralized employees. The previous VP had been an office dictator who at first seemed to be effective, but absenteeism, transfer rates, and low employee ratings across the entire department alerted upper management that there was a problem. Roger was eager to take on this new challenge, but he was understandably anxious.

He had attended one of my training sessions while working for his previous company and had seen for himself how effective Instant Influence could be. He called his new department together for a brief meeting at which he made several autonomy-reinforcing statements:

- "How things go here is ultimately up to you."
- "I'm going to introduce some new procedures that I'm really excited about, but you're the ones who are going to be using them, so I'm looking forward to hearing your feedback."

- "I know that things have not always gone so well in the past, but I'm looking for things to be different now. How willing might you be to give this new approach a try for a couple of weeks and then meet with me to tell me how it's going?"

Having set the stage, Roger then began inviting members of his department into his office for one-on-one meetings. With each employee, he had an Instant Influence conversation, focusing on what he had identified as his or her greatest problem area. Roger asked some why they might want to turn in weekly reports on time. He asked others what they might get out of attending biweekly meetings to talk about how the department was functioning. He even asked some employees why they might benefit from coming to work on time or from missing fewer workdays.

"It was rough going with some of them at first," Roger told me in an e-mail at the end of his first month. "But by now, I think we've got everyone on board. Absenteeism is down, the paperwork is getting done, our biweekly meetings are really productive, and you can just feel a difference in the whole office. What's really great is how contagious the whole process is. I tried to focus on only one issue per employee, but I've noticed that almost everyone's performance has improved. Someone I spoke to about paperwork is also coming in on time; someone who used to be out sick all the time has started turning in his weekly reports. I think people finally get the message that what they do here is up to them. Best of all, I think they've rediscovered why they got into HR in the first place. I know it sounds idealistic, but I think they're actually feeling good about helping people."

I was pleased to get Roger's e-mail because it reminded me why I got into this line of work as well. Using the six steps of Instant Influence really does inspire people to do their best.

Instant Influence at a Glance

Step 1: Why might you change? (Or to influence yourself, why might I change?)

Step 2: How ready are you to change—on a scale from 1 to 10, where 1 means "not ready at all" and 10 means "totally ready"?

Step 3: Why didn't you pick a lower number? (Or if the influencee picked 1, either ask the second question again, this time about a smaller step toward change, or ask, what would it take for that 1 to turn into a 2?)

Step 4: Imagine you've changed. What would the positive outcomes be?

Step 5: Why are those outcomes important to you?

Step 6: What's the next step, if any?

SUCCESS STORY: A CAMPING COMPROMISE

Every time I give an Instant Influence workshop in a business or professional setting, my trainees become excited for two reasons. They look forward to applying this approach in their professional lives, but they're also eager to take it home.

Tracey and Keith, in their early thirties, had been dating for about a year and had recently begun living together. I first met Keith at a workshop I was giving at Bristol-Myers Squibb, where he was a mid-level manager. He was so excited by my method that he decided to try it out on his girlfriend.

Keith was a real camping enthusiast who had always loved getting out into the wild. Tracey hated the idea of being anywhere without running water and a comfy bed. Keith thought she'd really like camping if she gave it a try, but he'd never been able to persuade her to join him.

It seemed the couple had reached an impasse. But here's what happened when Keith used Instant Influence.

KEITH: There's something I'd like to talk to you about. I understand that you've never liked the idea of camping. And obviously, I can't make you come with me. I know in the past, I've tried to do that, and I'm sorry. I get that it's your decision. *[Keith begins by acknowledging Tracey's resistance and reinforcing her autonomy, stressing that whatever she does is her decision, not his. This is crucial. Tracey will never be able to tap into her own reasons for going camping if she feels that she is just submitting to Keith's wishes.]*

TRACEY: Okay... *[Understandably, she is skeptical. They've had this fight a dozen times, and she doesn't believe that Keith is actually going to back off and let this be her choice.]*

KEITH: If I promise not to tell you what to do, will it be okay if I just ask you a couple of questions? We can stop anytime you want to, but I really would appreciate it. *[To further reinforce Tracey's autonomy, Keith asks permission to use Instant Influence.]*

TRACEY: Go ahead. *[If Tracey had not given permission, Keith would have had a few other options, which I explain later in the chapter. Tracey did give permission, so he was able to continue.]*

KEITH: If you were ever going to go camping with me — I'm not saying you are going to do it, I'm just saying *if* you did — what would be a reason you *might* do it? *[Step 1: Why might you change?]*

TRACEY: I don't know. To make you happy? *[Tracey still considers camping to be something that Keith wants, not something that she wants. But notice that she's not explaining why she doesn't want to change. She has at least begun talking about why she might want to change. The* might *is crucial, because it gives her an out, which, in turn, makes her less defensive. Lowered defenses leave room for Keith to influence her.]*

KEITH: Okay, well, on a scale of 1 to 10, where 10 is "I'd love to!" and 1 is "I don't want to at all," how ready do you think you might be to go camping with me next month? *[Step 2: How ready are you to change—on a scale from 1 to 10, where 1 means "not ready at all" and 10 means "totally ready"?]*

TRACEY: On a scale of 1 to 10? I don't know, maybe a 2. *[Tracey is being honest about how much she doesn't want to do what Keith is asking. But notice that Keith didn't ask her, "Are you willing to go camping with me?" If he had, Tracey would have just said no. Instead, Keith asked the question in a way that allowed Tracey to identify even the tiniest willingness to do what he wanted.]*

KEITH: Okay, 2, I hear you. But can I ask you something else? How come you didn't pick a lower number? *[Step 3: Why didn't you pick a lower number? Tracey expects Keith to ask why she isn't more willing to do what he wants. Instead, he's asking why she isn't less willing.]*

TRACEY: Why didn't I pick a *lower* number? I picked 2—that's pretty low!

KEITH: Yes, but you didn't pick 1. You could have said that you weren't willing to come with me *ever*. It's pretty cool that you're even a little bit willing to come. So I'm still wondering why you didn't pick a lower number. *[Sometimes you have to keep at these steps, finding new ways to phrase them or simply repeating them. Try to stay as calm and as neutral as possible. Remember, your goal is not to persuade the other person to do something or to point out where she is wrong. You want to let the other person discover her own reasons for doing something.]*

TRACEY: I don't know. I mean, I don't totally hate the idea of doing something with you that you like. It's not like it's always got to be my way. I just don't like not being able to wash my hands. *[Notice that Tracey is now starting to consider camping. However, she is still talking in terms of what Keith wants. Keith's goal is to get her to talk in terms of what she wants.]*

KEITH: I know you're always trying to make me happy, honey, and you know I appreciate that. But take a minute and picture it. If you *did* come camping with me—if you decided you wanted to—what *might* be good about doing that... *for you?* I mean, what do you picture? *[Step 4: Imagine you've changed. What would the positive outcomes be?]*

TRACEY: Well, you're always talking about how you love going to that place by the lake and waking up in the morning and making coffee on the fire. It would be nice having you make me coffee for a change! Hey, not having anything at all to do except be together would be pretty nice, too.

KEITH: If you decided you wanted to come—if I really wasn't forcing you, but you really wanted to—I would definitely make you coffee! I would cook for you the whole weekend. So why would having nothing to do but sleeping late and having me make you coffee and awesome food in a place I really like—why would that be important to *you?* *[Step 5: Why are those outcomes important to you? This one sometimes takes a little longer than the other questions. You often have to keep pressing until the other person gets to something that genuinely feels personal.]*

TRACEY: Look, if you really want to go camping, I suppose I could give it a try.

KEITH: Honey, it's nice that you're willing to try something I like. But I'm asking about what you want. Picture us on our camping trip, hanging out and looking at the stars, and eating all the great food I'm going to cook for you. Why would that be something you would want?

TRACEY: Why would I want it?

KEITH: Yeah. If you did want to go camping with me, why would those things you mentioned—having me make coffee and not having anything to do but be together — why would that be a *good* thing? *If* you wanted to do it?

TRACEY: I guess it would be important to me because it would finally be a chance to spend some time with you. We've been so busy that we haven't had any time lately to just do nothing, let alone look at the stars. So if the only way we can get that kind of downtime is camping, then I'll take it. But not for *too* long! You know, they have a lot of fancy camping equipment now. I'm sure you could make us a really nice meal. *[Tracey is finally talking about what is important to her.]*

KEITH: I'm sure I could. So . . . what do you want to do next? If anything? *[Keith could have stayed with Step 5 for a while, but he senses that Tracey is just about done with this conversation. So for now he moves on to Step 6: What's the next step, if any? Notice how he is leaving everything entirely up to Tracey.]*

TRACEY: Okay, honey. I didn't really understand how much this means to you. I still kind of hate the idea, but maybe we could go for one night. You do a lot of nice things for me. It would be nice to do something nice for you, too. *If* you cook for me. *And* take me somewhere really nice the day we get home. After I've had a chance to shower. *[Before trying this process, Keith had been so focused on selling Tracey on the joys of camping that it never even occurred to him to take another approach — offering to cook for her, taking a shorter trip, offering to take her somewhere she wanted to go in exchange. If he had tried to persuade her with those bargains, she might easily have balked, feeling pressured and pointing out that she was already making lots of compromises elsewhere in the relationship. But because she has offered this compromise, it feels very different to both of them.]*

KEITH: That's wonderful, Trace! Sure, we can go for one night. Do you want to help me pick the spot, or should I just do it on my own?

TRACEY: I guess you could show me the brochures or the maps or whatever. *[Now they've gone from Keith trying to get Tracey to come with him to her becoming actively involved in the planning.]*

Of course, the process doesn't always go this smoothly. But it's remarkable how much progress it allows you to make when you're trying to influence another person. The key is locating the tiniest spark of yes, even within a response that sounds like no.

IF THEY SEEM TO BE SAYING NO

"What if they just don't want to do what I'm talking about?" my trainees always ask me. "What if they pick 1 — 'not ready at all'? What if they just refuse?"

Initial refusal is not a problem. As long as you reinforce the other person's autonomy, as we saw in chapter 2, you can still begin the Instant Influence process.

HER: Look, I'm not going camping with you *ever*, so there's no point in asking.

YOU: Okay, I hear how much you hate the idea. Can I just ask you, though, might there be a reason you would ever want to go? Just in theory? And what is it?

HIM: I don't see why I should have to finish my homework before basketball practice.

YOU: I know doing homework before basketball practice has been tough for you. Just play along with me for a minute and tell me what *might* be good for you about getting your homework done that early.

HIM: There's no point in talking about this, because I really hate paperwork. I think it's a complete waste of time.

You: I totally get that. But would you mind considering just for a moment why you *might* want to fill out your weekly reports? What might be of benefit to you in filling out just one report, say, next week?

In any of these cases, you might convert Step 1 of Instant Influence into a question about having a conversation at another time, giving the other person as much decision-making power as possible: "Why might you want to talk with me about this another time?"

Once you have permission to proceed and have embarked on Step 1, it's usually best not to ask questions having yes-or-no answers: "Would you be willing to...?" "Could you consider...?" "Would you ever...?" "Isn't there just one reason...?" Saying no doesn't require much thought. And if you can't get someone to think, you won't be able to influence him.

Instead, begin Step 1 with questions such as "Why might you want to...?" "Why would you consider...?" "What benefit might it be for you to...?" Using plenty of conditional language (*would, might, could, perhaps, if, try, give something a chance*) prompts the other person to lower her defenses, increasing your opportunity to influence her.

Step 1 is also a version of the popular business approach known as WIFM — "What's in it for me?" Find a way to keep asking, "What's in it for you if you do this?"

The only time you should temporarily stop using the process is when the other person says, "I don't want to talk about this now." Do stop talking about it for a while, but make plans to talk about it later or just bring it up again yourself. Time and time again, I've seen the most profound changes occur precisely in these uncomfortable in-between places. And if you let the person walk away freely and on a positive note, there is a greater likelihood that the conversation will linger in her mind and continue to exert an influence. In contrast, pressing on might cause resistance. Your influencee might also surprise you and report that she has actually begun to change before your conversation is even finished.

In more than fifteen years of using this method and of hearing back from trainees and coachees, I know of only a few instances in which someone has offered a strong refusal. Even when people are reluctant, they usually have some willingness to engage in the Instant Influence process.

If They Really Don't Want to Change

Although it's rare for people to refuse to take part in the Instant Influence process, sometimes it reveals a genuine discrepancy: what the person has been saying she wants is not what she really wants. Perhaps your employee really doesn't want to support the goals of your company. Perhaps the negotiation can't succeed, the friendship can't last, and the couple has come to a parting of the ways. If so, this technique reveals the gap more vividly and with greater clarity than any other approach I can think of. A disgruntled employee may still be a bad fit, but after going through the Instant Influence process he is far more likely to see that and perhaps even leave rather than force you to discipline or fire him. A business deal may not be in both parties' best interest, a relationship may have reached its logical conclusion—but at least each side can come to that decision amicably and responsibly. Ideally, if you reach this type of impasse, you'll give the other person as much room as possible to identify the problem for himself.

INSTANT INFLUENCE STEP-BY-STEP

The Instant Influence process is an effective way to help people discover their own reasons for doing something—the most powerful motivators of all. Once you master the six steps, you'll be able to motivate just about anyone to do just about anything. Let's get started!

Step 1

Why might you change? (Or to influence yourself, why might I change?) I'm going to make a confession. Although ideally you would practice this process until it becomes natural to you, you don't need to do that. You could write the six steps on an index card and read them aloud or even put this book on your desk and read from it. In fact, we did an emergency room study in which patients underwent an Instant Influence "conversation" with a laptop that was programmed to respond automatically; the results were almost as good as when the conversation was conducted by a trained professional.[1]

But if, like most people I train, you don't feel comfortable doing something mechanically, and because you are likely to encounter a wide variety of situations and responses, here are some suggestions for how to vary and adjust Step 1.

• *Focus on the present: "Why are you currently doing [insert area of interest]?"* Sometimes, asking about a possible change in the future ("Why might you want to cut out sugar and eat more veg-etables?") seems like too lofty a goal. Instead, you can focus on something the person is currently doing and ask why she is doing it. ("Why did you choose salad for lunch today?") The GE execs I described in the introduction were understandably skeptical about my method, so I didn't want to begin by asking them why they might want to learn Instant Influence — that seemed to be too great a leap from where they were. Instead, I asked why they were there, why they had chosen to be present at that moment.

I've sometimes encountered objections to this "present-oriented" approach. Once I suggested to a frustrated manager that she ask her perpetually tardy staff member why he had arrived on time that day.

"But he was late every other day this week!" objected the manager. "He's *always* late! If I ask him why he was on time today, won't it look as though I'm praising him? Being on time occasionally isn't enough—I want him to be on time *every* day!"

I reminded the manager that her goal was not to win an argument or a power struggle but, rather, to motivate the employee to be punctual. The way to access his motivation, to get him to choose what she wanted for him, was to tap into his own choices. If he had chosen to come on time even one day, wasn't it worth asking him why? If he could identify why he had chosen punctuality today, perhaps he would decide to choose it more often, maybe even all the time.

Of course, people often deny that any choice was involved. They might focus on the how ("I just happened to catch the right train today"), insist that they were forced ("I'm here because I have to be"), or simply deny all responsibility for their actions ("I don't know—it just worked out that way"). It doesn't matter. You can respond by getting them to see that they have made a choice ("You say you have to be here, but not everyone in your department chose to comply with the memo. So why did you comply?"). You can also ask them what might be in it for them now that they have "accidentally" done something ("Okay, you just happened to be on time today. So what might you get out of that, now that you're here?"). You can also jump right to Step 2: "So on a scale of 1 to 10, how motivated were you to come in on time today?" However you begin it, the process will work equally well.

• *Focus on the past: "Why have you ever [done the thing we're talking about]?"* If there is no desirable behavior in the present to refer to and the future seems too daunting, perhaps there's something in the past. My colleague Andy, for example, was extremely frustrated with his inability to start an exercise program. "I just can't do it," he told me, very frustrated. "With the kids' baseball three nights a week, home improvement projects, this new course I'm teaching, and that new committee I'm on, I don't have the time, and I can't imagine that I ever will."

Andy, of course, was focusing on the how: "How, with all

the things that I have to do, will I ever find the time to exercise?" I wanted to avoid the dead-end discussion of my suggesting how he might do it. Instead, I asked him if there had ever been a time in his life when he had gotten regular exercise.

"Oh, yes," he said promptly. "When I was in college. Life was so much easier then — I didn't have all these responsibilities."

"Okay," I said, still trying to avoid the how. "Why did you want to exercise back then?"

He looked at me with annoyance. "I just told you. I had a lot more time."

"That's why you felt you *could* exercise. But why did you *want* to?"

Andy struggled a bit with the question but finally came up with an answer: "I used to go swimming every morning, and I'd have a real 'swimmer's high' afterward. It lasted the entire morning." Once Andy could access that initial motivation — the reasons he'd wanted to exercise several years ago — he could access why he wanted to exercise now, too, and we could move on to Step 2.

Not All *Why*s Are Created Equal

Be aware that some *why* questions can lead you to a negative place. Try to focus on the whole meaning of the sentence rather than on the word *why*.

*Why*s to Avoid	*Why*s to Rely On
Why don't you...?	Why might you...?
Why haven't you...?	Why would it be good for you to...?
Why wouldn't you...?	Why could it work for you to...?
Why can't you...?	Why might it benefit you to...?
Why shouldn't you...?	Why might you want to...?
Why couldn't you...?	Why might you decide to...?
Why aren't you...?	Why might you even think about...?

Reflecting Motivation

Now that you've asked your influencee some version of Step 1, you want to begin using a technique psychologists and counselors call *reflection*. As the word suggests, reflection is the process of repeating back, or echoing, what the other person has just said, as if you are holding up a mirror to his words.

Psychologists use reflection in many different ways, but our focus here is motivation. We need to reflect back even the tiniest spark of motivation to help the other person see more clearly what it is he already wants.

To achieve this, we may also have to reflect resistance or possibly frustration. Paradoxically, as soon as an influencee feels that his resistance has been heard and understood, he may drop some or all of it and become more cooperative.

Here's how a reflective conversation might go:

DANNY: I really should quit smoking.

YOU: So, it sounds as if you'd like to quit smoking. *[Notice how Danny used the word* should *and you chose* like to. *You're avoiding* should *because it sets Danny up for the law of psychological reactance. By using a slightly different phrase, you're still reflecting back what Danny said, but you're helping him get in touch with what he wants.]*

DANNY: Yeah, but I don't really have the willpower. I've tried before, and I've never been able to do it. I'm just not very good at sticking to the hard stuff.

YOU: You feel really frustrated about this, but you'd also like to be able to stop. *[You reflect the resistance. Danny is clearly frustrated by what he sees as his lack of willpower and persistence. But you end your statement by reflecting the motivation: if Danny had the willpower, he would stop; therefore, he would like to stop. You always want the motivation to be the last thing your influencee hears, because we tend to remember best the most recent thing we hear.]*

DANNY: I am pretty frustrated. These cigarettes are costing me a fortune.

YOU: So you might want to quit in order to save some money. *[Notice how your reflection focuses again on what Danny wants or might want. Someone engaged in pure reflection might simply rephrase Danny's remark, perhaps acknowledging the emotion: "You're frustrated about how much you're spending on cigarettes." But your focus isn't on how Danny feels so much as on what he wants, and that is what you are reflecting back to him.]*

Note that you're not putting words into Danny's mouth. He said he "should" quit smoking and that it's costing him a fortune. You are simply rephrasing his thoughts in terms of what he wants and why: "So you *might* want to quit smoking because then you wouldn't be spending a fortune and you could save some money." It's best to use conditional language if possible, to reinforce the other person's autonomy and leave him room to decide for himself.

Sometimes reflection involves acknowledging feelings, thoughts, and explanations that might upset you or with which you deeply disagree. Suppose your company has just extended the hours of its customer service line and is requiring everyone in your department to come in one Saturday a month. An employee says, "I hate this new policy, and, in my opinion, the guys in charge are just trying to load us up with busywork so we won't notice what a mess they've made of the company. The whole situation is completely unfair, and I shouldn't have to pay for it with my free time."

Perhaps you support the new policy; perhaps you even suggested it. You still might want to say to your employee, "I hear that you're really frustrated by this new policy. You think it's unfair, and you don't think you should have to go along with it."

Notice that you haven't agreed with your employee or admitted that he has a point; you've simply reflected back what your employee has said, just to let him know you've heard and understood him. But if you can honestly say, "You may have a point" or "You might be seeing something I haven't considered," you can create an opening for new, cooperative dialogue.

Ideally, your reflection should focus as much as possible on the positive. If the other person is really upset, with you or anything else, you may need to acknowledge these feelings as they surface. But do your best to reflect back even the tiniest hints of motivation as you hear them.

Getting to Maybe

Ideally, we'll use Instant Influence to move ourselves and others from no to yes. But sometimes we need to see the value in moving from no to maybe.

Suppose you are working with an assistant who balks at a new policy requiring employees to request vacation days three months in advance. Previously, only one month's notice was required. Your assistant is up in arms.

"Well," you say, trying to use Instant Influence Step 1, "why might you want to follow this new policy?"

"I don't want to follow it, and I don't think anybody in the company should follow it!" your assistant exclaims. "How in the world can you consider this a fair policy?"

Can you find the tiny opening in that seemingly all-negative response? The opening—the potential breakthrough—lies in the fact that your assistant is asking you a question. She isn't just saying, "No, I won't do it"; she's arguing with you. Of course, you'd like the conversation to end with her wholehearted agreement that the policy is fair or at least that she is fully committed to following it. But you might even be pleased if she only gets as far as, "I still don't like it, but it might not be as awful as I thought. I might follow the policy—I'll have to think about it."

Here's a fascinating finding from a key motivational study.[2] Hospitalized patients who wrote that they would definitely attend follow-up appointments at an outpatient clinic once they were discharged from the hospital were just as likely to blow off the appointment as the people who wrote that they definitely would not go. Who was most likely to show up? The ones who wrote that they might go. In that case, *maybe*—ambivalence—was even more powerful than *yes*.

Wrapping Up Step 1

People often ask me when it's time to wrap up Step 1 and move on to Step 2. They wonder how they'll know if they've gotten enough value out of the first question, and they worry that the transition to Step 2 might seem abrupt.

Just continue when you think the time is right, when you feel you've gotten all you can from this part of the process. If something isn't working any longer or never really worked, no worries—on to the next step! Focus on the questions that are working or that might work.

Don't be concerned about the transition, either. Just ask the next question. It may feel abrupt to you because you're aware that you're using a six-step process. The other person won't be thinking about it that way, even if you've told him exactly what you're doing. He'll simply try to give you an answer.

Before we move on to our review of Step 2, it's time for a little quiz. Here's your chance to find out how much you've learned so far.

Test Your Instant Influence Skills: Step 1

A member of your sales team has just flubbed a call, and you're trying to motivate her to call again. Three of the following statements are effective ways to influence someone; three are likely to generate resistance. Put a check next to the effective statements and try to define why they might work. Identify what seems problematic about the other three statements. Then read the answers and explanations below.

- ☐ I think your sales pitch just tanked. How do you think you're going to get that client back on board?
- ☐ Why might it be useful to call that client back and give it another try?
- ☐ Why don't you give that client another call?
- ☐ Why might it be beneficial for you to make a second call?
- ☐ How would it help you to consider making another call?
- ☐ Why don't you think about making another call tomorrow?

I think your sales pitch just tanked. How do you think you're going to get that client back on board? Not effective. This statement focuses on the how, not the why. Assuming you're correct and the employee did tank, asking how she's going to fix the problem may simply demoralize her. You'd be much better off helping her tap into why she wants to call again rather than inadvertently encouraging her to wonder whether she has the right stuff to close the sale.

Why might it be useful to call that client back and give it another try? Effective. You're encouraging your sales agent to explore her own reasons for making the call. If she knows why she wants to make the call, she'll have a much easier time finding the courage and determination that she needs to follow through.

Why don't you give that client another call? Not effective. This is a *why* question, but it's phrased negatively. It encourages your sales agent to rehearse the reasons she can't or doesn't want to call, rather than helping her to focus on why she does. It also sounds like a veiled way of saying, "You should make another call," which might trigger resistance.

Why might it be beneficial for you to make a second call? Effective. Phrasing the question this way spurs your sales agent to think about what she has to gain from the call, which is the most effective way of breaking through her anxiety and self-doubt.

How would it help you to consider making another call? Effective. This question likewise inspires your sales agent to think about what might benefit her, which should be enough to get her past her embarrassment and fear of defeat so she can make the call.

Why don't you think about making another call tomorrow? Not effective. As with the third question, this is a *why not* question that invites the agent to explain why she can't or doesn't want to make another call. It's a backhanded and somewhat manipulative way of giving her an order.

Step 2

How ready are you to change — on a scale from 1 to 10, where 1 means "not ready at all" and 10 means "totally ready"? The goal of Step 2 is to help you and the other person gauge his motivation. Often one or both of you will be surprised at how much more motivated the influencee is than expected. For example, after insisting that he doesn't want to stop instant messaging and texting during family movie night, your son responds to Step 2 by putting his readiness to change at "about 4." You would have guessed 2 or even 1.

If you are doing this process yourself — for example, to motivate yourself to get started on your taxes — you might be surprised to discover that your motivation level is as high as 6. Like the participants in Martin Seligman's study we learned about in chapter 1 — the depressed, exhausted people who suddenly found themselves happier and more energized—just thinking about why you might want to do something can inspire you to want to do it more.

However, don't attach too much importance to the numbers people give. A low number doesn't mean that they're not likely to take action, nor does a high number mean that they are likely to take action.[3] What's important isn't the number but the process of thinking about why they might want to do something.

It's worth remembering that we psychologists have never been able to design a questionnaire that could accurately predict how likely a person is to take action.[4] That's because, as counterintuitive as it seems, a person's stated level of motivation has almost no relationship to what he or she actually does. People who rate themselves 2s often go on to act, while people who rate themselves 10s often do not. So when the person you're speaking with says she's a 4, for example, don't get too concerned about whether the number is low or high. All you really need to focus on is her reasons for not choosing a lower number. Again, what produces change is not the size of the number but the process of thinking about the question.

"Do you think you'll ever get around to filing those weekly reports?" is a dead-end question, which may elicit such answers as "I'll try" or "I hope so" or (if she's being honest) "Probably not." But asking, "On a scale of 1 to 10, how motivated are you to file your next weekly report?" takes her out of the all-or-nothing realm and allows her to imagine a spectrum of possibilities. "Okay," the other person acknowledges. "I'm at least a little motivated to file the report."

Suppose you ask your wife if she would mind your skipping a weekly dinner with her family so you can stay home and watch a game. If you ask her flat out, her first response might very well be, "Yes, I'd mind. I'd rather you come with me." She's unlikely to say, "I don't know" or "I can imagine it being okay under some circumstances, I guess," because that's not where her mind goes when you ask that yes-or-no question. Her brain simply hears, "Yes or no?" In this case, the answer is no.

What if instead you said, "I'd like to run something by you. There's something I'd like to do, and I want to get a sense of how you feel about it. On a scale of 1 to 10, how ready do you think you might be to let me off the hook this Sunday so I can stay home to watch the game?" Now your wife has to think about it. How important is this dinner to her? How ready is she to let you stay home? Maybe more ready than she thought. What does she think when she imagines you not being there with her? "Well, I'll be a little bit embarrassed showing up without him...but come to think of it, I'd love to have some time alone with Mom, and I love playing with Sue's new baby, and I can't really do that if I have to make sure my husband's having a good time." At least now she's thinking about the possibility of your not coming, instead of simply dismissing the idea. And even if she says, "The answer is 1 — I'm not ready to do that at all," you can still respond by asking, "Okay, I hear you. So what would it take to change that 1 into a 2?" Instead of giving you a yes-or-no answer that she has to defend, she's actively thinking about letting you skip the dinner. And she's telling you what it would take to change her mind.

If she truly hates the idea of your missing the event, this process isn't going to change those feelings. In fact, she may realize why your presence is so important to her, and the two of you may have a totally different conversation about your place at her family functions — a more heartfelt and less defensive conversation than any other you've had so far. You may even discover that you don't mind going, now that she's speaking from the heart rather than insisting on her due. But if there's any part of her that really wouldn't mind, this way of asking gives her room to find it. You both avoid a power struggle. And now the conversation can begin.

Don't Break the Dead Man's Rule!

There's an old saying in counseling: Don't try to motivate anyone to do anything that a dead man could do just as well.

For example, we never try to break through resistance to get people to not drink or stay away from fattening foods or stop getting in your own way. A dead man doesn't drink, he never eats fattening foods, and he's long past getting in his own way.

Instead, we might try to move someone to refuse the next drink or to stick to healthy meals and snacks or to call up that company to ask for a job interview. Now the person has an active role to play— something he needs to be alive to do.

When you ask people why they might want to do something or how motivated they are, you're asking them about behaviors, not outcomes. Most of the time, we can't control outcomes, but we can control behavior. We can't commit to losing weight, but we can commit to sticking to a meal plan. We can't commit to getting a job, but we can commit to making ten job inquiries by the end of the week.

It's also useful to focus on the next step rather than on the final step: "I'll stop texting and instant messaging during the next family movie night" rather than "No cell phone or computer ever during special family times." Some people I've trained have objected to this "baby-step" process, feeling that I'm asking them to be too easy on their influencees. But we only get somewhere by taking one step after another, and having taken the first step, however small, we almost always find ourselves motivated to take the next one. Trust the process, try to remain open to the idea that any problem can be solved, and let the process work for you—one step at a time.

Step 3

Why didn't you pick a lower number? (Or if the influencee picked 1, either ask the second question again, this time about a smaller step toward change, or ask, what would it take for that 1 to turn into a 2?) Because people are used to being pressured and badgered into doing what other people want, they're often surprised to be asked about what they want. With this question, we're saying, "Okay, some part of you wants to take this action. What's that part about?"

Some of my trainees wonder if this question validates the other person's weak motivation. "What if asking that question drives the number down even lower?" one sales manager asked me. "What if someone says, 'Wow, you're right. That number *should* be lower!'"

These concerns, while understandable, miss the point. The number isn't important. As we learned earlier, the number doesn't even predict how likely someone is to actually do something.[5] What is important are the person's reasons: Why are they even a little bit interested in doing what you're asking them to do? Inviting them to engage in that thought process — no matter which number they choose — is the best way for them to discover how much they really want to take action.

Test Your Instant Influence Skills: Step 3

You're still working with the sales agent who flubbed the call. She admits that her motivation to make the call again, on a scale of 1 to 10, is only about a 3, but you feel that you're making some progress. Even so, you find yourself asking lots of questions that you realize aren't very effective. But you do ask one effective question.

Look at the following questions and check the one that works. Then think about why that question is likely to spur someone to action while the other three are more likely to promote increased resistance.

☐ Why haven't you called back already?
☐ Only a 3? Why aren't you more ready to call back than that?

☐ Why haven't you given up completely?

☐ How are you going to prepare yourself for the next time you call?

Why haven't you called back already? Not effective. This question invites your sales agent to rehearse her reasons for not making the call. It immediately puts her on the defensive because the wording suggests that she should have called them back. Maybe so, but if she's feeling defeated or anxious because of her previous failure, this question won't help her access the determination she needs to make a second call.

Only a 3? Why aren't you more ready to call back than that? Not effective. Again, asking your sales agent why she isn't more ready to do what you want her to do immediately puts her on the defensive. The question isn't why she's *not* ready to call back. The question is why she isn't *less* ready to call back.

Why haven't you given up completely? Effective. You and your sales agent are still discussing the possibility of her making the call. That means she must want to make the call, at least a little. Focusing on why she wants to follow through will help her—and you—fan that little spark of desire to make the call.

How are you going to prepare yourself for the next time you call? Not effective. This might be a terrific question after your sales agent has committed to the next call. Once she is drawing on the powerful energy of *why*, she may indeed benefit from talking about *how*. But until she is deeply committed to making the call, asking her how to prepare for it will only remind her how unprepared she currently is.

Step 4

Imagine you've changed. What would the positive outcomes be? The first three steps of Instant Influence are primarily designed to establish a few initial reasons for change. Sometimes these reasons are very powerful and motivating. Other times, the reasons people give are relatively trivial or superficial, but that doesn't matter in the first half of the process. Just reaching a point where it's clear that someone might want to change is good enough.

Steps 4 and 5 are intended to help your influencee deepen his commitment. They're based on the premise that the strongest reasons for change are the most personal, and they're designed to ferret out those deeply held reasons that may have never been consciously articulated but are there nonetheless. The key to Step 4 is to help your influencee visualize a change that has already taken place, not one that he is in the process of making.[6] A completed change can feel satisfying or exciting; a change in the offing may sound like a lot of hard work, which could discourage your influencee before he even begins. So make sure Step 4 evokes a strong sense that the change is already a done deal.

Here are some suggestions for how to rephrase Step 4:

"Imagine that you've already made the change we're talking about. Now tell me how you'll benefit from that."

"Let's say it's three weeks from now, and we've brought in that consultant I'd like to hire. She's done her work, submitted her report, and you're looking it over. What good things might come of that for you?"

"Suppose we waved a magic wand and this change just happened—no cost, no effort, it's just magically done. How would you benefit?"

You can suggest that the change has already happened, describe the change yourself, encourage the influencee to visualize the change in detail, pick a date by which the change will be complete, or fall back on the idea of a magic wand or effortless transformation (which helps take the focus off the how and the belief that it can't be done). The goal is simply to make the outcome real to the other person, so he has an opportunity to recognize how much he wants it.

Staying positive is also key. Ask about the potential outcomes of positive behavior. Research has shown that people are far more likely to change if they think of the upside of changing, rather than the downside of not changing. For example, in a recent study of 170 smokers, conducted by a former intern of mine and his colleagues, smokers who were asked to consider positive messages about quitting smoking ("If I stop smoking, my clothes will smell better, my family will spend more time with me, and that will make me feel good") were nearly three times more likely to achieve six consecutive weeks of abstinence than were smokers who were asked to consider negative messages about continuing to smoke ("If I don't stop smoking, I may get cancer, my clothes will continue to smell, and my family will spend less and less time with me because of the secondhand smoke").[7]

Of course, if your influencee can't identify any positive outcomes, then you can take the opposite tack. Ask him to imagine things staying exactly as they are for, say, the next three weeks, and then ask him to describe the possible outcomes of that. Even if his focus is on the negative, however, you should continue to present his responses in a positive way:

INFLUENCEE: If I keep on like this, I'll gain even more weight, and I might have a heart attack like my father did.

INFLUENCER: So you're thinking that changing your diet might help you lose weight and keep you healthier, so that you could avoid the terrible consequences of your father's illness. Changing your diet means that things could be much better for you.

91

Step 5

Why are those outcomes important to you? This step is where you encourage your influencee to dig as deep as she can for the most personal reasons to take action. Recall the beginning of this chapter and the way Keith continued to ask Tracey about why she wanted to go camping with him. Talking about making Keith happy or even about him cooking for her were not nearly as personal as when Tracey talked about wanting more downtime together so they could focus on each other. It took Tracey a while to discover those reasons within herself, but when she did, she was not only willing to go camping, she was actually excited about it.

We don't need our influencee to be as enthusiastic as Tracey became, but we do want her to find a reason that she really clicks with. "I'd like to spend less time on Facebook during my workday because I really have a lot to do" isn't nearly as personal as "If I spent less time on Facebook, I'd finish my work by five instead of six, and I could beat the rush hour driving home." And that is still not as personal as "If I spent less time on Facebook, I'd get home in time to take a nap" or "I'd get home in time to play with my daughter" or "I could use that time to call my brother — I never talk to him anymore, and maybe I could work in a fifteen-minute call once in a while." The more personal our reasons for doing something, the more likely they are to be important to us, and the more effectively they'll move us to take action.

It may take you some effort to get to the truly personal reasons, which are often quite surprising. Usually, the responses that people begin with in Step 5 are the more conventional ones: "to keep my job," "it's good for my health," "so I can get into college," "I owe it to myself," "I have to do it," "I should do it," and so on. It can take a little time, trust, and creativity to get to the heart of the matter, but that is where real change happens. Be persistent.

One technique that my trainees and I have successfully used

is an approach I call the "five whys." You start by asking, "Why are those outcomes important to you?" For every answer you get, you repeat the question, until you've asked it five times. Invariably, the answers move almost magically from the practical and impersonal to the heartfelt and deeply personal. As the questioner, your role is to keep eliciting more personal answers; if you hear a response that seems to be "other directed," say something like, "Duly noted, but what about for you?"

Here's an example in which Nathan, a middle manager in the sales department of a large corporation, talked about why he wanted to adopt a new departmental procedure that would require him to meet more often with the members of his sales team. Initially, Nathan, like most of his colleagues, felt deeply resentful of the procedure, but by the time he'd reached Step 5, he had begun to get behind the new approach.

INFLUENCER: Okay, so imagine that you've adopted the new approach and three weeks have passed.

NATHAN: I guess the department would be running more smoothly.

INFLUENCER: That's great, but that's for the department. What about you? Why would that be important to you? *[Step 5, first why]*

NATHAN: Well, of course, if the department is running more smoothly, I guess I'd be happier.

INFLUENCER: Why would a more smoothly running department be important to you? Why would that make you happier? *[second why]*

NATHAN: Because things have been pretty tense, so it would really be a welcome change.

INFLUENCER: Why would things being less tense be a welcome change? *[third why]*

NATHAN: Well, everyone else would be having a better time. That would make me feel good.

INFLUENCER: Why does it make you feel good when other people in your department are having a better time? *[fourth why]*

NATHAN: We'd all get along better.

INFLUENCER: Why would it be good for you if you helped the department get along better? *[fifth why]*

NATHAN: You know, all my life, I wanted to be a leader—I mean, a real leader—someone who really sets the tone and gets things going. I always thought I had it in me. But I always pulled back. I hate to say it, but I think it's because I was so pissed at my dad, who was always kind of passive, you know? He never really stepped up, not like I thought he should have. Maybe I haven't, either. Maybe now, with this new approach, I could.

I realize that Nathan's response sounds almost too good to be true. Why would a business guy at a training with his colleagues suddenly start talking so personally about his father? But this is the kind of emotional, heartfelt response that I've seen people give to that fifth why, time and time again. I've seen it from tough, cynical probation and parole officers, skeptical CEOs, and burnt-out ER staff, and everyone is always surprised by the deeply personal discoveries they and their colleagues have made. After having witnessed it so often, I'm no longer surprised, though I am always moved. That's why I believe so deeply in the power of *why*. I'm pretty sure that after you've tried the "five whys," you might begin to believe in it, too.

Selective Reflection

At this point, when you reflect people's statements back to them, you want to focus even more specifically on motivation than you have thus far, omitting almost entirely any mention of resistance. By the time they've reached Step 5, people don't necessarily need to hear echoed to them all the ways they are feeling uncertain, angry, or upset. Rather, they need to hear how they're hopeful, what they want, why they want it, and how they truly believe things could be better—particularly if their faith, hope, and desire are buried so deep within that they aren't even aware of them.

Sometimes, through the reflection process, it's useful to summarize the progress you've both made, though gently, so as not to trigger the law of psychological reactance. As always, use lots of qualifiers and leave room for the possibility that the person you're speaking with sees it differently. For example:

> So if I understand you correctly, even though when we started you weren't so sure about this new office procedure, now you are saying that it could really benefit you. *[Pause here, and count to "five-Mississippi" before speaking. Then, if there's no answer, ask:]* Does that sound like an accurate summary of what just happened?

Finally, try to reflect back the most personal and compelling motive for change, which is usually the response to the fifth *why*. For example:

> It sounds like you might want to stick to this new office policy so that you can prove that, unlike your dad, you've become a real leader—a strong, positive example for your team.

Step 6

What's the next step, if any? Finally, we're no longer asking for the whys of change; we're asking for the hows: "What's the next step, if any?" Adding those two little words at the end is another way to reinforce the other person's autonomy: it's still up to her to decide whether there will be a next step. This may be the moment to press for a commitment to change, or attempting to do so now might be premature. (In part III, I'll help you figure out how to evaluate your results, talk you through the process of making an action plan, and help you identify those situations in which change simply isn't going to happen and you need to move on.)

Fortunately, some kind of change is usually possible, even if it takes more than one Instant Influence conversation to get there. So don't worry if Step 6 takes a little extra time to bear fruit. As we saw in chapter 1, an Instant Influence conversation might lead to complete commitment, partial commitment, or simply a new openness to consider the issue. Even when someone commits to change, it may take some effort to figure out exactly how to put that change into action.

Often, though, people who reach Step 6 are eager to make big, sweeping changes, which leads them to promise a lot. "Okay, Dad! I've been bad about taking care of Spot in the past, but I'm going to feed him every day from now on." "Wow, now that I see how much time I've been wasting on Facebook, I'm never going to be on it for more than fifteen minutes a day." "Those closets are going to be all cleaned out by Sunday, and they're going to stay that way — period."

Whether you're influencing yourself or someone else, take change slowly. Support the enthusiasm, but pick a next step that is smaller and easier to fulfill. "How about feeding Spot every day for the coming week, and then we'll check in and see how it's going?" "I'll try a thirty-minute workday limit on Facebook with unlimited time there on weekends. In a month, I'll review." "I'll clean the hall closet by Sunday, and the bedroom closet the week after that. Then I'll figure out what to do about the storage closet."

Influencers might be tempted to skip Step 6 if the next step seems obvious. However, if you think the other person is ready to identify the next step, keep going. You may think you've heard someone already state his next step, but he may not have heard himself say it. You might also have misheard or misunderstood. Even if the other person has named the next step, the worst that can happen is that he'll hear himself express it even more emphatically ("I already *told* you, I'm going to feed Spot every day").

That goes for you, too, by the way, if you're trying to motivate yourself. Make sure you say out loud or clearly write what your next step is going to be. Even if you know what it is, you'll feel far more motivated if you articulate your plan.

Now that you know how to use Instant Influence, you'll be able to try it out in many different situations: by yourself, with people who say they want to change, with people who say they don't want to change, even with strangers such as clerks, waiters, and customer-service people. In part II you'll find out how to apply this process most effectively.

PART II

Expanding Your Influence

CHAPTER FOUR

Influencing Yourself

I f only we could influence ourselves the way we can others! Sure, it's easy to see what someone else could do differently, but it always seems much harder to apply those same lessons to ourselves. As you've thought about ways you might use Instant Influence to help colleagues, employees, family members, and friends, maybe you've found yourself wishing that someone would come along to influence you.

The good news is that you can use the Instant Influence technique on yourself as easily as you can use it on someone else. Because this process depends on a series of specific steps designed to tap into your inner desire for change, you don't need a skilled therapist or even an insightful friend to get you started. You can influence yourself.

Often, you'll discover that your true motivation is quite different from what you thought it was. My writer-friend Yvonne had that experience when she decided to use Instant Influence to work on her writer's block.

Yvonne has been a professional freelance writer for many years, and she takes great pride in meeting all her deadlines.

With the clients she likes, she often starts the job early and finishes early, leaving herself time to do the things she loves — seeing movies, meeting friends, and exercising.

With the clients she doesn't like, however, she puts off starting work as long as she can and then finishes at the last minute, which results in lots of unnecessary stress. She also deprives herself of any fun she might have had in her spare time, because she can't enjoy herself with deadlines looming.

So when Yvonne started using Instant Influence to end her procrastination, she thought she knew what her reasons would be: "avoid all that stress," "feel pride in my work," and "have more time to myself." But what came up instead was revenge. As she wrote out the Instant Influence questions and her own answers, she found herself writing,

> Bette *[a client she didn't like]* has already gotten enough out of me — she's not getting ONE MORE MINUTE. She's already made me miserable enough — well, no more! I'm going to finish this stupid assignment and then go out to a movie, damn it!

To Yvonne's surprise, this revenge motive actually worked, and she found herself writing up a storm. She did indeed finish her work early, and she was rewarded with both professional pride and a touch of glee.

"I don't know why I didn't realize how I felt before," she told me. "Maybe I felt guilty about disliking her so much; I don't know. But finding out why I *really* wanted to finish that assignment — and therefore start it as early as possible — helped to remove the block. I wouldn't have suspected it in a million years, but there it was."

The Process at a Glance

1. Identify a change you'd like to make or an action you'd like to take.
2. Formulate it in terms of behavior, not results: "I want to follow my eating plan for two weeks," rather than "I want to lose weight."
3. Write down the first Instant Influence question (Why might I change?), and then write down your answer. Try to write as quickly as possible when you answer, without stopping to censor or question your responses. (You can do this exercise on a computer or longhand, but sometimes the physical act of writing evokes deeper thoughts and feelings.) Write as much as you like. Don't worry if you seem to wander off topic. When you feel as though you're finished with the first question, move on to the next, and so on, until you reach Step 5.
4. When you get to Step 5, write "Why?" then answer. Repeat four more times so that you've asked and answered the "five whys."
5. If at any point you have trouble completing an answer, find a slightly different way to ask the question. (Review chapter 3 for suggestions, if necessary.)
6. When you reach Step 6, choose a small, manageable step, and pick a time that you will check back in with yourself to review your progress and choose a next step.

Note: If you're comfortable talking to yourself, you can also do this process orally, perhaps recording yourself. Just write down your next step when you reach Step 6. I encourage you to either write down the answers or say them aloud, however—don't just think about them. You'll have more influence on yourself if you can actually read or hear your own reasons.

WHEN YOU'RE HAVING TROUBLE TAKING ACTION

Sometimes we use Instant Influence on ourselves, and the process progresses swiftly and easily. Other times we have trouble getting started. Still other times we may even find ourselves procrastinating about using this technique. If you feel stuck in any area of your life and you're finding it difficult to begin the Instant Influence process, here are a few suggestions that might ignite a spark.

• *Start small.* Thinking of the smallest possible action needed to begin a task can make the task seem a lot more manageable. Writing a quarterly report may seem daunting—jotting down a single sentence, not so much. Paying your bills might sound exhausting—placing your checkbook next to your computer, a breeze.

My colleague Marcus was having trouble motivating himself to call his tech-support guy to begin the long, complicated process of upgrading his computer and learning a new operating system. Every time he thought about calling the man—a simple enough task on the surface—he pictured the hours and days and weeks involved in choosing a new laptop, ordering the software, working with the technician to set up the system, and mastering the technology. Daunted by the prospect of so much work, uncertainty, and frustration, Marcus never managed to make the call. He couldn't even persuade himself to begin the Instant Influence process, which he had successfully used before to take up running.

Finally, he mentioned the problem to me. I suggested he scale back a bit. "Don't focus on calling the techie," I said. "Think instead about finding the guy's number, writing it down, and putting it by the phone."

Marcus couldn't believe that such a simple shift would make a difference, but he agreed to give it a try. Instead of asking himself, "Why might I want to call my tech guy?" (Step 1) and "On a scale of 1 to 10, how ready am I to call him?" (Step 2), he wondered, "Why might I want to look up my tech guy's number and put it by the phone?" and "On a scale of 1 to 10, how motivated am I to find and display the number?"

Once Marcus focused on smaller steps, he found himself beginning to move. And once he started moving, the momentum continued. One day, he looked up the number and put it by the phone. The next day, while reaching for the phone to make a doctor's appointment, he saw the number, and, as he told me later, "I just ended up calling without even realizing I had done it." It's as if Marcus had been creating his own psychological reactance by telling himself he *had* to call the tech guy. In order to remove the block, he needed to give himself some autonomy reinforcement: "I don't have to call the technician. I could just look up his number."

Remembering this experience, Marcus tried focusing on tiny, beginning steps all the way through the process: not on installing the new software, but just taking it out of the box; not on reading the instruction manual, but simply placing it near the computer. Every time those baby steps did the trick. Once he'd made even the least bit of progress, his natural motivation took over and carried him along.

• *Imagine how many different ways you could approach your problem.* Sometimes, as we saw in chapter 3, we tend to get hung up on the how. We become convinced that there's only one way to reach our goal, and then we obsess about all the obstacles that prevent us from doing that.

But often, as Keith and Tracey learned, there are many different ways to solve a problem, some of which sound more appealing, more feasible, or just plain easier than the one on which we've become stuck. Tracey couldn't imagine going on one of Keith's regular camping trips, but she was happy to plan a "luxury" outdoor overnight, with Keith cooking for her and later taking her somewhere special. Likewise, a colleague of mine loathed the thought of reading some business books that I had recommended to him, but he brightened when he realized that he could listen to the audiobook versions while on a long drive to visit relatives.

When we use Instant Influence with other people, we tap into their autonomy as well as their creativity by inviting them to come up with their own solutions for their own problems. We can do the same thing for ourselves. Allow for the possibility that any problem might have many different solutions. Perhaps even challenge yourself to come up with some alternate solutions without considering whether they'll work. You might discover that contemplating crazy, humorous, or obviously unworkable solutions can trigger a new idea that is actually quite practical.

• *Allow for the possibility that every problem can be solved.* Resistance doesn't just block us from taking action; sometimes it also keeps us from thinking. Even when we try imagining how many different ways we could approach a problem, we might become despondent if ten or fifteen minutes of concerted effort don't provide us with an answer. "There is no solution," we tell ourselves, and our motivation fizzles.

It doesn't have to be that way. We can commit to the possibility that every problem can somehow be solved. We might need to change the ground rules or redefine the problem or redouble our efforts or expand our search for resources, but at the very least it's possible that somewhere, somehow, this problem has some kind of solution.

To find that solution, we must vow to keep an open mind. It can be tempting to let your motivation fade away, but try to resist. If the possibility of a solution is real to you, you'll be eager to stick with the process, which in turn can motivate you to keep searching for the solution you need.

• *Be ready to be surprised!* One of the great gifts of Instant Influence, as my friend Yvonne found out, is the way it so often surprises us with new insights about ourselves. Our newly discovered motivations frequently take on a momentum of their own, and soon we are accomplishing prodigious feats, sometimes in quite unexpected ways. "Oh," you might say to yourself, "I had no idea I thought that. I had no idea I wanted that. I never would have expected to find myself doing that."

I can't count the number of times I've begun the Instant Influence process and seen the influencee laugh in amazement, shake his head in wonder, or absorb a new insight in silent awe. So go ahead. Think of something you'd like to do that has been difficult for you; find a small, doable first step; and use Instant Influence. Almost certainly, you'll motivate yourself to take action. You might also learn something new about who you are and what you can accomplish.

Focus on Action, Not Decisions

When we're trying to change, we often feel overwhelmed by the prospect of a huge, life-altering decision or even a small but difficult decision. The key is to use Instant Influence to help you take action, not make a decision. If you want to make more time for your family, bypass the life-changing decision ("I'm going to reprioritize my life and shift my focus from work to family") and focus instead on having a five-minute conversation with each family member, once a week. If you are thinking about changing your eating habits, ignore the big-picture decision ("Am I ready to commit myself to being healthier?") and just ask yourself why you might want to add fresh fruit or vegetables to your weekly diet. Choose something that you can literally see or hear yourself doing (an action) rather than something that remains in your mind only (a decision or a new way of thinking).

What I love about big life-altering decisions is that, eventually, we are led to them—gradually and sometimes without our knowledge—through our actions. Allow yourself to focus on behavior, and your decisions will take care of themselves.

Test Your Instant Influence Skills: Choosing a Manageable First Step

You're preparing to influence yourself, but you're having a hard time getting started. Rephrase each of the following Step 1 questions (Why might I change?) as a smaller, more manageable step:

- Why might I want to stick to my eating plan for life?
- Why might I want to exercise half an hour every day?
- Why might I want to get my taxes done next weekend?
- Why might I want to spend more time with my family?
- Why might I want to give myself more time to relax?
- Why might I want to organize our home filing system?
- Why might I want to pay all our bills on time?
- Why might I want to apply to graduate school?
- Why might I want to answer all my e-mails within a day of receiving them?
- Why might I want to go through my closets and give away clothes I no longer wear to a thrift store?

Possible responses:

Why might I want to stick to my eating plan for life? "Why might I want to make a shopping list in case I ever wanted to shop for my eating plan?"

Why might I want to exercise half an hour every day? "Why might I want to lay out my exercise clothes near the bed?"

Why might I want to get my taxes done next weekend? "Why might I want to put my W-2 forms on my desk?"

Why might I want to spend more time with my family? "Why might I want to spend half an hour reading to my daughter?"

Why might I want to give myself more time to relax? "Why

108

might I want to take five minutes when I get home from work to shut myself in the bedroom and just breathe?"

Why might I want to organize our home filing system? "Why might I want to buy some colored file folders next time I'm at the mall?"

Why might I want to pay all our bills on time? "Why might I want to put all the bills in a single pile the next time I'm watching television?"

Why might I want to apply to graduate school? "Why might I want to look at one grad school's website?"

Why might I want to answer all my e-mails within a day of receiving them? "Why might I want to answer two e-mails today?"

Why might I want to go through my closets and give away clothes I no longer wear to a thrift store? "Why might I want to look up the phone number of a thrift shop?"

SUCCESS STORY: AN ASSISTANT AT LAST

I was giving a workshop for treatment providers, probation officers, case managers, and staff from Connecticut's Department of Children and Families. As part of the training, I had everyone do a written, self-administered version of Instant Influence so they could see firsthand just how powerful this process is. Most of the time, I pick a current concern in my life and do the process along with everyone else, but this time I thought I might just catch up on some paperwork.

No dice. The state professionals in my session weren't going to let me skip any part of the training that they had to do. And many of them were still openly skeptical about what I was proposing. Clearly, I had to comply with my own request or I'd lose all credibility.

I decided to focus on something I was then wrestling with: hiring a new personal assistant. Although Yale provides me with an assistant for university business, I thought I should hire someone privately, too, to help manage all of my consulting jobs.

Somehow, though, I had never gotten around to taking action. I kept telling myself that a good assistant would be too hard to find, too hard to train, and too expensive. As the months wore on, I had just about convinced myself to give up the idea. Now I decided to consider it again, and, for the first time, I used the Instant Influence process to do so.

Of course, the law of psychological reactance applies to me as well as everybody else. So I had to give myself some autonomy-reinforcing statements. "You don't have to do anything," I told myself firmly. "You're not really doing this process. You're just going through the motions, for the training." (This "out"—telling myself that the process didn't count—has proven to be a very useful way of bypassing resistance, and I heartily recommend it to you.)

On to Step 1. How would I formulate my first question?

First, I reminded myself that I needed to focus on behavior rather than on results. I couldn't commit to hiring a personal assistant or even to finding one, since neither of those outcomes was in my control. I had to commit instead to looking for one.

The action of seeking a personal assistant, however, seemed dauntingly vague, especially since I was so sure that I would never find one. I told myself that I could focus on a simpler action, such as advertising for a personal assistant. But even that step seemed too big.

Trying to remain open to the idea that any problem could potentially be solved, I decided to start as small as possible. If I wanted to hire a personal assistant, what was one small, non-threatening step I might take?

I randomly brainstormed ideas and made a list:

- Post the position online somewhere.
- Look into where to post the position.
- Write a job description.
- Choose the salary I would pay.
- Figure out how many hours the assistant would work for me per week.
- Google some job descriptions for personal assistants so I can write mine more easily.

That last option felt right to me. "Why might I want to google some job descriptions for personal assistants?" Yes, that seemed like a nice, safe step. It didn't commit me to much, and I could sort of imagine doing it.

So if you're wondering how you'll know if the baby step you've settled on is the right one, here are two hints: it feels safe, and you can visualize yourself doing it. When we haven't done something before, we often feel some resistance. Choosing a safe step is a way to trick yourself into making the process seem easy.

Sure enough, as I began thinking about my newly formulated Step 1 ("Why might I want to google some job descriptions for personal assistants?"), I came up with an answer that had somehow never occurred to me: "Because if I did hire a personal assistant, I might get someone really good." *Wow*, I thought, surprised already. I never imagined that.

I began jotting down the six steps of Instant Influence, as well as my answer to each question. Here are the initial notes I made:

Step 1: Why might I want to google some job descriptions for personal assistants?

- I might get someone good.
- More time with my family.

What's interesting is that this last very good reason did not even occur to me until I gave myself permission to focus on the small action of googling job descriptions rather than the big action of actually hiring someone. Notice, too, how I had somehow already jumped past the idea of googling job descriptions, or even writing and posting a job description, and had moved on to the prospect of actually hiring an assistant. Starting somewhere—in effect, tricking myself into picking one small step—had really given me momentum.

Step 2: On a scale from 1 to 10, how ready am I to do research on Google about how to hire an assistant by Friday?

8 [my first response]
7 [what I went with]

Notice how I spontaneously jumped ahead, already planning to hire an assistant and even giving myself a one-week deadline to do it. Of course, this was pretty unrealistic, especially since I don't have control over all the factors involved in hiring someone, but that's the sort of excitement that can emerge when you start using Instant Influence. While you're doing the first five steps, just let yourself write without censorship or judgment. You're trying to get in touch with *why* you want to do something. You can scale back your plans, if necessary, when you get to the how in Step 6.

Step 3: Why didn't I pick a lower number?

- I might really be able to hire someone!
- Who knows what will come of it?
- I want to do it.

- It could make me less anxious about all the things dangling here and there.
- It could free up so much time.
- It's not *that* expensive.
- It could be fun.
- Things could get more organized.

Again, my answers didn't always make logical sense, and I was still being rather unrealistic about how quickly I could get everything done. But that's okay. This is the time to write whatever comes to mind. I could wait until Step 6 to consider the practical side of things.

Step 4: Imagine it's happened. What are the positive outcomes?

- I could focus more time on intellectual activities.

Here is where I really started to get excited. I started to imagine that hiring a personal assistant would free me up to concentrate on writing, giving seminars, and speaking about Instant Influence to groups — all things I love — because someone else would be taking care of the organizational details that I'm not so crazy about. Notice that I couldn't let myself feel this kind of enthusiasm when I was still trying to force myself to "hire an assistant" or even to "write an ad." I had to trick myself into entering the process, focusing only on googling potential job descriptions. Now I was feeling how much I really wanted an assistant, how good it would be for me to have one. All my concerns about training and paying an assistant and figuring out the logistics had taken a backseat to my new motivation to find and hire the person who would free me to do the work I love.

- Time for more gratifying aspects of my work.
- Makes me want to organize everything.

This was another unexpected reaction. The whole point of having a personal assistant was that I wouldn't have to think about the organizational details. But suddenly I was getting excited about working with this person to organize my work better, even though I'd have thought that would be the last thing I wanted to do.

- I'd get paid sooner.

A personal assistant could make sure my clients got billed right away. She wouldn't put off that work the way I often do.

- I may actually find someone good.
- Reassurance.

This was a brief note, but I remember what I thought as I wrote it: *If my kids are sick, I can still get some work done; things won't grind to a halt.*

- Tax break.
- Get more work done.
- Help with travel.
- Expense reports.
- Claims.

Now I was moving into the kind of detail that I would actually want to put in a job description, listing the tasks that I might expect a personal assistant to do. Interestingly, by Step 4 I had already begun taking action to get an assistant, writing the job description that only a few minutes ago had felt mind-bogglingly difficult to even consider.

- Dry cleaner, car wash, child care, other life scheduling.

I was also learning more about what I wanted in an assistant. I didn't just want the kind of administrative help I'd had through my department at Yale. I wanted an all-around personal assistant who could help me with many tasks in my life.

Step 5: Why are these outcomes important to you?

- Helping someone in this really bad economy!
- Might help another person get into my field.

These were completely new ideas to me. I had never before thought that hiring an assistant might be of benefit to someone else. I really liked that idea, and I was struck, once again, by how Instant Influence opens up motivations that are indeed important to us but that we somehow never knew we had. Our motivations may even tap into our deepest purposes or into our desire to help others. For some reason, these altruistic motivations are frequently the most hidden — and the most powerful.

- Sidelined ideas will get attention.
- Work getting done while I'm not working.

That was my favorite! I loved the idea that my assistant and I would be working at different times, but that the work would somehow always continue.

- Spend more time with family.

Step 6: What's the next step, if any?

At this point, the time I had allotted for doing this exercise was over, and the people I was training were about to reconvene.

So my next step became, "Tell the group." When I did, three people in the audience immediately offered to take the job!

I didn't end up hiring any of them, but I took the experience as a sign that the whole process of finding an assistant might be a lot easier than I had thought it would be. Certainly, now that I was motivated, it would be easier than it had been.

Later that week, I had a very frustrating meeting about a university project I'd been coordinating for a while. I found myself at a local Starbucks before having to go to another meeting, and I really wanted to clear my head and change my mood. "Let me just do some kind of work that feels satisfying," I told myself, and I ended up writing a job description and posting it online without really intending to do so. Within forty-five minutes I got my first response—and she was indeed the young woman whom I hired.

As the process came full circle, my new assistant wrote an e-mail to the group of trainees who had pushed me to join them in the exercise, introducing herself and thanking them for their role in creating her new job. She was happy, I was happy, my family (with whom I did indeed have more time) was happy—and I had seen once again the power of Instant Influence.

Improving the Process

- Keep looking for smaller and smaller beginning steps until you find one that feels safe or that you can at least visualize doing.
- Don't judge or self-censor. Just be open to the process.
- Explicitly remind yourself to ignore the hows and why nots. Focus instead on *why* you want something.
- Expect to get carried away. The tiniest step often sets in motion a series of thoughts, feelings, and ideas that create new momentum.
- Prepare to be surprised. You will almost certainly learn something new about your own reasons for wanting something.
- Trust the process. You may find yourself taking action almost without realizing it, so don't feel you need to force yourself.

INFLUENCING "OUTSIDE THE BOX"

People in my workshops often ask me about how illogical, odd, or even "weird" the Instant Influence questions tend to sound. Believe it or not, that's part of the point. Research suggests that when people are presented with illogical, odd, unrelated, or irrational material—in scientific terms, "meaning-threat" material—they tend to arrive at better solutions in less time. Apparently, we work harder, faster, and better if our natural motivation to make sense of things is stimulated before or during a problem-solving task.

In 2009, researchers Travis Proulx from the University of Southern California at Santa Barbara and Steven Heine from the University of British Columbia conducted a study in which forty college students were asked to solve a puzzle.[1] Half the students were given an absurdist short story by Franz Kafka to read before the task; their work on the puzzle was significantly more accurate. On average, they did more than 60 percent better than the other students. Being prodded ahead of time to think "outside the box" was good for their problem-solving skills—and I think it might be good for yours, too.

Often, when we're trying to solve a problem we rule out some possibilities prematurely or miss options that we forgot, didn't notice, or didn't take seriously. We get hung up on looking for immediate results, focusing on how to do something rather than on why we want to do it, or allowing temporary setbacks to prove to us that we'll never be able to get what we want.

Instead, trust the process. Stop asking yourself, "Is this possible?" and start asking, "Why do I want this?" Shake things up by deliberately focusing on behavior that seems less realistic or even downright unworkable.

I once tried to help a colleague, a budding research scientist, get a job at another institution. She couldn't seem to focus on the job search for positions that would have been appropriate for one with her credentials, so I suggested she motivate herself to try for a project manager's job, which was technically out of her league. "Why might I want to look for a job at the project manager level?" was her Step 1, even though she knew she didn't have the credentials to get that job.

Yet somehow, finding out how much she wanted something she knew she wasn't qualified to pursue made her want the jobs that were appropriate, and her job search suddenly—and very successfully—took off. Asking irrational questions and considering illogical actions isn't necessarily the best plan of action. But it can be a terrific way to stir things up a little and to find the motivation that you need.

A colleague who had gotten divorced about a year before was having trouble motivating himself to date again. He had even tried using Instant Influence but felt that it hadn't really broken through his frustrations with the dating scene.

I suggested that he, too, try a somewhat irrational approach. Perhaps his Step 1 might be, "Why might I write out a description of my dream partner and look through an online dating service for someone who matches that description exactly?"

My friend understood that this narrow focus wasn't necessarily the most mature or productive approach to dating. He might meet someone—on a dating service or somewhere else—who didn't precisely conform to every item on his dream list, someone who nevertheless might make an exciting, supportive, and loving partner for him. But giving himself permission to be childish and irrational freed his mind, and he found himself understanding far more clearly just what attributes did matter to him. Contrary to his initial fantasies, he knew he didn't really need his potential match to be stunningly beautiful, a fabulous cook, or a die-hard sports fan. What he did care about, he discovered, was finding someone who was caring, passionate, and devoted to him, while still being independent and dedicated to her own career.

Armed with this new clarity and focus, my friend was able to write a better ad for himself and do a far better job of reviewing the ads of potential dates. More important, he also found himself keeping an eye out for that type of woman during his daily life—a proactive, optimistic approach to dating that had previously seemed beyond his reach. He hasn't found her yet, but he's enjoying the search more than he ever thought he would, and, from where I sit, he's looking in a way that guarantees him the best possible chance of finding what he wants.

STAYING TRUE TO OUR HIGHER PURPOSE

One of the things I'm always struck by is how often people assume that our deepest, truest motives are selfish ones. The desire to do something for someone else—whether a loved one, a stranger, or the community—is somehow more suspect than the wish to do something purely for oneself.

After decades of using the Instant Influence technique myself and with others, I've found that our deepest motives are not always the selfish ones. Sometimes our true wants spring from our highest, most noble ideals as we desire the best for our families, friends, neighbors, and fellow citizens. Sometimes, too, we can't truly grasp our real reasons for doing something unless we are open to the generous, community-minded nature of our deepest desires. As you're thinking about what you want most and how to inspire yourself to go after it, stay open to the possibility that in doing so you're looking to help others as well.

CHAPTER FIVE

Influencing People Who Want to Change

I f someone wants to change but hasn't done so yet, turn first to the Instant Influence process. Reinforce his autonomy, do the six steps, and work with him to make an action plan. (We'll cover action plans in detail in chapter 9.) Most of the time, this works, but what if it doesn't? What if someone says he wants to change but doesn't seem to be taking any action? What if you yourself are trying to take action but can't quite get started?

In my experience, there are three main reasons why seemingly motivated people get stuck:

1. They lack the skills they need to move forward.
2. It's the wrong time or situation in which to take action.
3. They haven't identified their true desires.

SKILL VERSUS WILL

As we've seen, we often focus too much on the how when we really should be looking at the why. But sometimes the how is the problem, and acquiring skills may be all that's needed to get the ball rolling.

How can you tell whether the issue is skill or will? Following are a few questions to help you figure it out. You can use them to determine whether you should attempt Instant Influence for a first or a second time, or whether you should instead focus on helping your influencee acquire skills. You can ask these questions of anyone: a colleague, an employee, a loved one, even yourself.

• *Do you have the information and training that you need?* If we want to make changes but haven't yet taken action, perhaps we simply don't know what to do. We might lose motivation as a result, but as soon as we get what we need our enthusiasm returns.

• *Have you consulted an expert?* Experts may be able to identify whether the problem is one of skill or will. They also might be able to help you or your influencee acquire any necessary skills.

• *Have you already focused on the skill?* Consider a supervisor who identifies a troubled employee's problem as a lack of skill and sends her to an in-service training. If the employee returns newly confident in her abilities and motivated to work well, skill was clearly the problem. But if she comes back frustrated and demoralized or displays an initial burst of enthusiasm and then becomes discouraged, chances are that will is playing a role. One option is to send her to another training after using Instant Influence to motivate her to engage in it more fully. Or you might switch gears and focus instead on the employee's motivation, using the Instant Influence process to address her most challenging behavior.

WRONG TIME, WRONG PLACE

Usually, if we really want to do something, we find a way to do it or at least take the first step. Yet sometimes a person may genuinely want to take action but also may have very good reasons for not doing so. Before making any assumptions about his motivation level—and before jumping in with Instant Influence—ask yourself these questions.

• *Is this the right time for him to take action?* Occasionally, external factors force us to reorder our priorities. One of my colleagues, for example, was highly motivated to enroll in an advanced Spanish class with the goal of conducting studies in South America during her next sabbatical.

Then her husband's father got cancer, and she felt as though her life had been turned upside down. "My priorities are my courses, my kids, and my father-in-law," she told me. "I've put my research on hold, along with activities at church and pretty much everything else. I'm not going to think about getting back to normal until three months after he's done with radiation—and even then, I'll have to see."

Of course, this is an extreme example, but it makes a point: sometimes even the most powerful motivation takes a backseat to a new, more pressing set of priorities. My colleague was genuinely motivated to improve her Spanish, but she chose to wait before acting on that intention. At the time, other matters were more important.

If this sounds like someone you know, ask periodically about his intention to make a change. Then use your instincts to evaluate his responses. If what you hear is a motivated person making clear choices and setting appropriate priorities, all is well; do nothing. If he seems to be in conflict, ask permission to engage in an Instant Influence conversation, and see if you can help him get back on track.

• *Is he already getting additional training or doing some internal work?* Progress isn't always obvious, even to ourselves. It's possible that we are motivated to do something but are genuinely not yet ready to begin — not because we've reprioritized, as my colleague did, but because we're preparing ourselves at a level that we simply can't see. Motivation is like a seed that sprouts and begins to grow while still underground. We may know it's there, but we don't always trust that one day it will break through to the light.

In some cases, we may be fully aware that we need more training or experience, and we are consciously working to acquire those skills and credentials and emotional preparedness. Our supervisor, colleagues, friends, or spouse may not realize what we're doing, because we're deliberately keeping our preparation under wraps or are just not making a fuss about it.

In other cases, unbeknownst even to ourselves, we may be silently preparing for a new challenge. We've tapped into our motivation and know what we truly want, yet on the surface nothing has changed. It will take time for the seed we planted to sprout and bear fruit; until then, it remains hidden.

If this sounds like someone you know, ask whether she's ready to start on the change she's mentioned. If she seems calm and comfortable with the question, she's probably on the right track. If she seems upset, agitated, or shut down, consider asking her permission to engage in an Instant Influence conversation, to spark her motivation.

• *Has he begun to pursue a new goal or to make a change in a way that isn't obvious to me?* Sometimes we expect people to announce to us what they're doing; sometimes we even expect that of ourselves. Think for a moment about changes you've found yourself making without quite knowing how they started, of transformations that seemed to happen by themselves, and of all the times that you were changing in ways that others didn't realize. Often, change is only obvious after the fact.

If this sounds like someone you know, look as objectively as you can at the person's actions, and ask yourself what they add up to. You may be surprised to see that, contrary to what he may say, change is taking place. If you feel change is not taking place, consider having an Instant Influence conversation, but remain open to the possibility that changes that you cannot see may be happening.

• *Has he suppressed his motivation because of how little autonomy or how much confrontation he has experienced?* This can happen to any of us when others are threatening our sense of emotional safety. Nobody likes being told what or how he should think and what he should do. No matter how motivated we are to act, too many threats to our autonomy are liable to trigger the law of psychological reactance, making it virtually impossible for us to access our motivation.

If this sounds like someone you know, make it your top priority to restore the other person's autonomy. Commit to accomplishing that first rather than trying to get the person to do a task or make a change. If she is ever to access her true motivation, she must genuinely feel that it is *her* motivation, not something imposed on her by someone else.

If Someone Has Tried and Failed

Sometimes a person who is genuinely motivated to take action loses faith in herself. She may simply need encouragement. Here are some autonomy-reinforcing ways to express your belief in someone:

• You're obviously very motivated to change, because here we are talking about it. Since you want things to be different, they certainly can be. If you decide you want to do something, you can definitely do it.

- If you could do this thing that you feel you can't do, would you want to do it?
- Let's not worry about how others view your success or failure— let's focus on what you want and why you want it.
- For now, let's not address your desire to figure out what's realistic. Let's just look at what you want.
- I believe that you can change your future if you get motivated, so let's work on that together, if that's what you want.

ACCESSING YOUR TRUE DESIRES

One key aspect of Instant Influence is the amazement people feel when they hear themselves say that they want to do something for a reason they'd not yet identified. People who are openly resistant say they don't want to change, but then they surprise themselves when they discover that they do. They're even more surprised when they realize why.

But what if you already know you want to change and even know some of the reasons? ("I need to get more organized, or I'll always be stressed!" "I want to do my homework, Dad, because I know good grades are important—I don't know why I never seem to get around to it." "I really want to catch up on those e-mails—I hate to keep people waiting.") You might have to look a little deeper to find the surprising truth that will really move you to action.

This was the experience my writer-friend Yvonne had, as we saw in the previous chapter. She was highly motivated to get her work done on time, and she thought she knew why (professional pride, to have more free time, to avoid stress). In fact, her real reason—revenge—lay deeper. She had to reflect a bit longer to discover that.

But perhaps the problem lies elsewhere. Perhaps we really don't want what we thought we did. Perhaps we wanted to advance as far as we could in the company; now we just want more time with our families. Perhaps we dreamed of going to grad school; now we want to switch careers entirely.

Sometimes we invent a false desire in order to avoid a real problem. Instead of confronting our boss about a coveted promotion, we fantasize about going into business for ourselves—and then never quite get started on a plan. Instead of addressing a problem in our marriage, we focus on how much we want children—but somehow never manage to schedule an appointment with the fertility doctor. Our problem is not a lack of motivation but a lack of clarity.

Occasionally, we take on the wishes of people around us—parents, partners, even friends—instead of acknowledging our true desires. We believe in those false dreams, then wonder why we can never seem to take action to make them come true. All too often, our true desires scare us, either because they seem difficult to attain or because achieving them would shake things up elsewhere in our lives.

In each of these situations, our challenge is to discover what we truly want. If you say you want something but find yourself feeling stuck—before or after you've used the Instant Influence process—the next exercise might help you figure out what you really want. And the answer might surprise you.

What Do I Want and Why?

Allow at least half an hour of quiet uninterrupted time to complete this exercise.

1. Identify something that you would like to do—a specific concrete action. If your goal is to lose weight, you might choose something like "follow my eating plan for a week." If your goal

is to stop being late, you might choose "to be on time for my next three appointments."

2. Find a blank piece of paper and something to write with. (You can do this exercise on a computer if you prefer, but there is something about the physical effort of writing that taps more deeply into our innermost thoughts and feelings.) Write the following question: Why would I like to [your goal]?

3. Answer as quickly as you can. Don't stop writing until you have filled up the entire page. If you run out of things to say, keep rewriting your last word or sentence until you have moved on to a new thought. If you don't know what to say, write "I don't know what to say" and keep doing so until you have a new thought. Alternately, ask yourself why you might benefit from the last reason you wrote down, and then write about that.

This is a useful exercise for accessing thoughts and feelings you didn't know you had. You may find this technique particularly effective when you are using Instant Influence on yourself and you reach Step 4 (Imagine you've changed. What would the positive outcomes be?) or Step 5 (Why are those outcomes important to you?).

THE TYRANNY OF *SHOULD*

Sometimes a person who really wants to change is trapped by shoulds. As we've seen, the autonomy-reinforcing part of Instant Influence and the "five whys" (see chapter 3) are designed to help clear out shoulds, leaving only compelling personal reasons for taking action.

A colleague struggled with grading student papers in a timely fashion. We began an Instant Influence conversation during which he offered me a long list of reasons for his difficulty. Personal feelings were intermingled with a liberal help-ing of shoulds: professors should get their work done on time; students should be treated with respect; the dean had a right to expect him to fulfill his obligations; his colleagues had to turn in their grades on time, so he should, too. We finally filtered out the obligations to discover his true motivation for grading papers on time: helping students understand how to express their ideas in writing, so that one day he could welcome them as colleagues in his field.

"If that was your only reason, you probably would have got-ten your grading done on time every single semester," I told him.

"Then why haven't I done it?" he asked.

I laughed. "Because of all those *other* reasons!" It wasn't that the other reasons weren't valid. They just didn't hold deep, per-sonal importance to him, even though he thought they should.

Don't Take the Bait

Here are some phrases that I always listen for during Instant Influence conversations, so I don't get caught in the *should* trap. Be especially wary if the person says he should do what *you* think he should do, such as enter a treatment program or, in the case of my sons, do his homework before basketball practice. I've learned not to take these superficial shoulds as the true reasons that will produce real and last-ing change.

Don't accept reasons that include the following phrases:

- I should...
- I know I should...
- I wish I could...
- I ought to be more responsible because...
- It's expected of me...
- Others would feel [how] if I didn't [do what].

Test Your Instant Influence Skills:
Identifying an Obstacle

Think of three people you know, perhaps including yourself, who have said they want to change but can't. For each person, identify one reason you can't see any signs of change:

- They lack motivation.
- They lack skills, resources, or assistance.
- They have other priorities that are genuinely more important to them.
- They're in the process of acquiring skills, resources, or emotional readiness.
- They're changing in ways I don't recognize.
- They don't really want to make the changes they're supposedly committed to.

After you've identified a potential reason each person may not be taking action, identify how you might best help them. Your answers might include:

- Help them get the skills, resources, or assistance they need.
- Support them in their current efforts.
- Help them identify what they really want.
- Have an Instant Influence conversation with them to help them take action.

It can be challenging to hear people say they want to change and then watch them do nothing to achieve their goal. Try to stay calm and detached. One of the first lessons a therapist has to learn is not to want more for the patient than he wants for himself. It's also an important point to remember when using Instant Influence.

KEEPING YOUR PERSPECTIVE

One of my greatest challenges when helping people get motivated is resisting my impulse to steer them toward actions that I think they need to take. When you're dealing with people who have drug addictions, alcohol problems, eating disorders, or grave psychiatric issues, it's tempting to think you should just sell them on the course of action that you know they need, especially when they keep telling you how much they want to change.

The problem with this impulse, though, is how much frustration and even anguish it can cause. I know that a problem drinker should get treatment, and it breaks my heart when he doesn't agree. I'm sure that a habitual drug user should enter the rehab program I've found for her, and then I'm disappointed when she refuses to go. Pretty early on in my life as a therapist, I realized that I had to come up with another approach. Otherwise, I'd burn out completely, and I wouldn't be helping my patients, either.

A doctor needs to understand that her job is not to save her patient but rather to help him make the most well-informed decision possible. Otherwise, the doctor becomes locked in fruitless argument, trying to convince an ever more resistant patient to do something that he stubbornly refuses to do. Only by fully committing to the patient's autonomy and genuinely believing that "everyone already has enough motivation" can the doctor help the patient choose his own path, which might or might not include the treatment that the doctor considers best.

Helping my influencees make the most informed decision. I realized that had to be my motivation, and I invite you to consider whether it should be yours, too. Whether you're helping someone with drug addiction or homework, anorexia or sales protocols, you may find it easier and more productive to focus on a goal that respects the other person's autonomy and helps you accept the limits to your power.

CHAPTER SIX

Influencing People Who Don't Want to Change

When I teach the Instant Influence method to people accustomed to dealing with difficult clients and employees, I often hear a lot of objections. "Oh, sure," they'll say, "this works great on people who are already motivated and just need to tap into it. But you should see the people *I* have to deal with. This will never work on *them*."

When you're dealing with resistant people, it can be hard to believe that this or any other approach is going to help. Some people seem adamant in their refusal to change, and perhaps also in their resentment, frustration, and apparent indifference. But I promise you that Instant Influence works, very nearly 100 percent of the time.

If you're still feeling skeptical, keep in mind that I'm the one who gets the impossible cases: the longtime alcoholic who's "flunked out" of every rehab; the homeless person addicted to heroin who's sitting on a gurney in the ER; the three-hundred-pound compulsive eater who's never been able to control his food intake. If Instant Influence works with people like these, it can work with the resistant people in your life, whether they're colleagues, neighbors, or loved ones.

An added benefit of Instant Influence in the workplace is that it does far more than enforce compliance. It also helps people discover their own reasons for working hard, following company rules, and making positive contributions. Instead of an employee who is a drudge, doing the bare minimum to get along, you get an actively engaged employee with a genuine, personal commitment to the job.

Still skeptical? As we learned in the introduction, my father is one of the most stubborn, determined people I've ever met—and, believe me, his son is the last person he'll let tell him what to do. Yet I was able to use the Instant Influence approach to help him decide to quit smoking, something that he maintained he had absolutely no interest in doing.

SUCCESS STORY: KICKING A HABIT

My father had been a lifelong smoker. When he was in his seventies, I worried about him. He had recently been struggling with all sorts of new health problems, and the need for him to quit smoking seemed urgent.

It's not as if I hadn't tried to get him to quit before. As a child, I actually hid, destroyed, and threw out his cigarettes. As a young adult, I pleaded with him—when I wasn't making demands or lecturing. As a middle-aged man, I resorted to angry, sarcastic comments, especially when I had to remind him that I didn't want him smoking around my kids. I tried "tell and sell" and countless high-threat messages; if there had been a few other misguided ways to approach my father, I'm sure I would have tried those, too. The only approach I hadn't tried was Instant Influence. By the time I developed it, I was just too angry to use it.

One day my wife and I brought the kids out to visit my parents. We had just finished a nice lunch, then, as usual, my father lit up.

My heart sank. I was so concerned for him. I thought I might have finally grown up enough to be able to confront him calmly, using the approach that I had come to trust.

But this was my father, the most stubborn man I knew. He never listened to anybody, least of all me.

Still, I had created Instant Influence to help people act on the goals that were really important to them. And what could be more important than good health? I loved my father, and I wanted to help him, so I plunged in.

"Dad, I'm concerned about your smoking."

My father was immediately on the defensive. "Is this what you came here for? Leave me alone. We all gotta die of something!"

I knew that one of the most important aspects of Instant Influence was establishing respect for the other person's autonomy, especially when dealing with someone who insists that he doesn't want to change. I knew, too, that for the process to work—for my dad to discover his own personal reasons to quit smoking—I had to be up front about my agenda even while I reinforced his right to make his own decisions.

"No, Dad," I replied carefully. "I didn't come here intending to have this conversation. But I'm concerned about you. I know I've badgered you about this in the past, but today I have a different question, if you don't mind..."

My father was having none of it. "Why does everyone get on my case about smoking?" he exclaimed. "I don't want to be bothered with even one question!"

Although I respected his autonomy, I wasn't going to let him get away without a fight. "Just one question," I pleaded, "and I'll leave you alone. You don't want to be badgered, and I understand that. So just let me ask one question, then, I promise, I'll stop. I won't bring this up again for the rest of the visit."

My father sighed loudly. "Go ahead," he said in the voice of a long-suffering man. "Hit me with your best shot."

I took a deep breath. "If you ever were to decide to quit — and you don't have to, Dad; it's your choice. But if you *were* going to make that choice, what would be the reason?" (Step 1: Why might you change?)

My father pointed to the pack of cigarettes that was close at hand, as always. "You know how hard it is to stop these things?"

Aha! The first spark of motivation. To most people, that might sound like arguing, like complete unwillingness to change. But after years of working with Instant Influence, I could hear the tiny opening that my father had just given me.

"So," I said quietly. "I hear you saying that you would quit if you could. It's just hard."

My father thought there might be a trick in there somewhere, but he couldn't tell what it was. "Yeah," he agreed grudgingly, "and I've tried to prove how hard it is to you, but you just don't understand."

"I do understand," I said. I remembered that I was supposed to reflect, both resistance and motivation. "You're saying that it's hard to quit, so you feel you can't do it, even though you might want to. But I asked you a different question. What I asked is, *why* might you quit, if you were going to? I'm not asking about how hard it might be but, rather, about what would get you to do that. What would be your reasons?"

My father was back to being annoyed. "Would you leave me alone, then, if I finally quit?"

"Oh, Dad, you know I'm never going to leave you alone. But that's beside the point. What would be a personal reason for you to quit smoking — one that matters not to me, but to you?"

"You think I like getting up every morning, coughing

my brains out?" my father said. "Believe me, I wish I didn't have to."

Despite my father's initial unwillingness, we had crossed an important line. Before, he'd said he didn't even want to talk about quitting. Now he was saying that he wanted to quit but felt he couldn't.

"So," I said, continuing to reflect back the motivation, "one reason you would want to give up smoking is that you'd feel better and you wouldn't cough so much."

"I guess."

"Okay, now, wait a second, Dad. I said I'd ask you only one question and then stop if you wanted me to. So is it okay if we continue?"

Dad sighed loudly again. "Yeah, whatever," he said. This was important. I knew that to deal with a person who insists he doesn't want to change, permission and autonomy are key. I had to keep getting Dad's permission to continue; otherwise, he could say I was badgering him, and he'd be right. I could see that he was slowly but surely getting in touch with his own desire to quit. But if I were to force him to have the conversation, all he'd ever feel was how frustrated he was with me and my desires and wishes. He'd never find the motivation he needed to make this change.

If he hadn't given me the okay to continue, I would have kept my promise and not brought up the topic again on this visit—though I might have gotten his permission to bring it up again another time. More likely, I would have simply waited for a different occasion, but I would have asked his permission at that point, too.

I went on to ask another question, a version of Step 2: How ready are you to change—on a scale from 1 to 10, where 1 means "not ready at all" and 10 means "totally ready"? I decided to pick the smallest possible reduction in smoking as the change I would ask about.

"Okay, Dad," I said. "Here's a really hokey question. How ready would you be to give up just two cigarettes a week?"

"Hey," said my father, "if I was gonna quit, I'd quit all the way. I either do something or I don't. That's how I do things. I'm a man of action."

"I believe you," I said, continuing to reflect what he had told me. "And I know it's hard. So if 1 means 'not ready at all' and 10 means 'totally ready,' how ready are you to give up just a couple of cigarettes per week?"

"Just two cigarettes per week wouldn't be hard at all!" my father insisted, totally switching ground. "I could do it. I'd say I'm a 6. Maybe even a 7."

"Okay," I said, moving on to Step 3. "Why didn't you pick a lower number?"

"What do you mean, a *lower* number? I thought you wanted me to do this!"

As you can see, each time I asked one of the questions, my father was a bit thrown. Sometimes he was confused, sometimes he was surprised, sometimes he just couldn't follow what I was asking. That's part of the power of Instant Influence, especially with resistant people. By shaking them out of their normal ways of thinking, it allows them to see things in a new light and perhaps get in touch with some feelings, thoughts, and desires they didn't realize they had. Clearly, my father did want to quit smoking. He just didn't think he could, and he definitely didn't like the idea of me pressuring him into doing it.

"We're not talking about what I want," I reminded him. "You picked a 6 or 7, so I wondered why you picked those numbers and not one that was lower."

"Well, that's easy," my father said scornfully. "Because it's gonna save me a little money if I stop smoking. Even if I just cut down one or two cigarettes a week." He paused to think about that idea. "If I ever did want to quit, that would sure be an easier way to do it. Cutting it down, little by little. . . . I bet I wouldn't even feel it." Ironically, if I had started simply by advising him to cut down gradually, Dad would almost certainly have rejected that idea the way he'd rejected all my other antismoking suggestions. He didn't need my advice—he needed to get in touch with his own reasons for cutting down.

Time for Step 4: Imagine you've changed. What would the positive outcomes be? "So, Dad," I said. "Let's imagine that when we all come back to visit you next month, you're smoking eight fewer cigarettes a month. You've done it, and it went well—"

Before I could even finish the sentence, my father cut in. "I could do a lot better than that!"

This is something I've noticed quite often with people who say they don't want to change. Once they discover their own motivation to behave differently, they have to find a way to prove to themselves that it was their idea all along. Frequently, they do this by upping the goal. You ask for the report by Friday, and they get it to you by Wednesday. You suggest writing one job application letter, and they write four. Or, in my father's case, I suggest eliminating two cigarettes per week, and he insists that he can cut back even faster.

"Okay," I said. "However many you would like to cut—what if you were able to do that?"

My dad was doing the calculations in his head. "I could get down to half a pack," he said.

"You seem excited about that," I commented.

"Ah, I'm not sure I'm really gonna do it."

"Well, *imagine* it's done. Imagine it's one month from now. What do you picture?"

Dad looked down at the cigarette in his hand. "I wouldn't be smoking right now," he said, almost ruefully.

I brought in Step 5 (Why are those outcomes important to you?). "You wouldn't be smoking right now," I repeated. "Why would that be good for you?"

There was a long pause. I had to draw on all my training not to speak. Instead, I counted silently, *one-Mississippi, two-Mississippi, three-Mississippi,* using the silly syllables as a way to force myself to keep quiet, so that Dad could have as much time as he needed to wrestle with this problem on his own.

Finally, he said, "Because I'd be in my backyard with my grandsons right now, instead of making the poor kids wait so I could have another cigarette."

Two Steps Forward, One Step Back...

In the space of a seven-minute conversation, my father had moved from total resistance to the powerful discovery of his most important reason to quit smoking. As soon as he stopped arguing with me about badgering him, he had the chance to realize how much he wanted to give up the habit that kept him from his grandsons. And his own reasons enabled him to act.

At the same time, my father, like many people who are reluctant to change, wanted to regain control of the conversation. So when we progressed to Step 6 (What's the next step, if any?), he found a way to make the goal his own by putting me down. "My friend told me about this new medication I should take to quit smoking," he said. "I'll ask my doctor about it. Why didn't you tell me about that medicine, Michael, since you're so smart? How come you didn't let me know, since you're a big psychologist at Yale?"

I bring this up not to criticize my father—who went on, with characteristic stubbornness, to cut back and eventually quit smoking—but to alert you to this possibility. Be prepared for all sorts of criticism and negativity, even if positive action is also taken. Of course, you might receive gratitude, appreciation, and admiration. But more likely, along with positive results, you will also get one or more of the following:

- Reminders that they, not you, had the idea that created the influence.
- Insistence that they will do this their way, not yours.
- References to your failures, shortcomings, or mistakes.
- Criticism of something else you've done that they don't like, to offset the productive conversation you just had.
- Accusations that you could have motivated them to change sooner but because of incompetence or bad faith, you withheld your help from them.

If you're like most of us, you'll want to protest, argue, or set the record straight. Try to avoid these very understandable reactions, and keep your eye on the prize. Someone who has refused to change is now planning to change. Even if he won't acknowledge your part in it, ultimately you will benefit.

REINFORCING AUTONOMY IN RESISTANT PEOPLE

As we saw in the example with my father, reinforcing autonomy is key with resistant people, but it's often hard to do. I still sometimes catch myself wanting to argue, to be right, or to simply lash out in frustration. But I remind myself that none of those responses will help turn the situation around. Reinforcing autonomy will—or at least it might. (For more on reinforcing autonomy, see chapter 2.)

Below are some suggestions for how to go about reinforcing resistant people's autonomy. Not all will be appropriate in every situation. Choose the ones that you feel you can say honestly and repeat sincerely before, during, and after the Instant Influence process.

- *Affirm their right to say no:* "It's totally okay if you don't do this."

- *Affirm their ownership of the decision:* "It's up to you." "This is your decision." "You're the one who will be living with your decision."
- *Denigrate the message:* "Even though the company wants it this way, and this is the standard we're all held to, I can see how you might say this isn't the best way..." "Maybe you can find a different way that works for you and doesn't have any negative repercussions for the company. I'd like us to talk about following the company system, and I'd like you to do it, but I can understand that you think it's not so great."
- *Denigrate the messenger (i.e., yourself):* "You're the machinist, I'm not. I just administer the conditions in which you do your work. I have no way of knowing how to do what you do." "I've been in your same position. Someone has told me, 'You have to change this,' and I've thought, 'I know how to do my job!'"

WHAT ABOUT THE CONSEQUENCES?

Consequences tend to be a frequent concern in my workshops. "I can't just let my employees do whatever they want," a trainee might protest. "If someone doesn't meet our company standards, shouldn't there be consequences?"

Parents have similar thoughts, as do frustrated spouses, doctors with resistant patients, and parole and probation officers. They all want to be sure that they're not avoiding responsibility or letting someone walk all over them. They can't quite believe that reinforcing autonomy and letting people make their own decisions can really have a good outcome—at least not with the difficult people they know. So they always ask, shouldn't there be consequences?

"Of course," I say. "And if someone insists on doing

something against the rules or something you really don't like, you always have that option.

"But if a fear of consequences was going to motivate the person you're talking about, he'd probably already be doing what you want him to do. Fear of consequences isn't nearly as powerful a motivator as knowing your own reasons for doing something. So for as long as you think there's hope of getting through, which almost always takes longer than you want it to, stick to the Instant Influence process, and deal with any consequences later."

If you must mention consequences, I suggest you do so *after* the Instant Influence conversation has gone as far as it can go—ideally in a separate conversation but at least after you've finished Step 6 (What's the next step, if any?). For example:

"How we move forward is up to you. You've heard me say what I think should happen next. What I want more than anything else is for you to be invested in your own reasons. But I'm not the only one involved in this process— I have supervisors, too, who may have their own ideas about what should happen."

"What happens next is your decision. But every decision has consequences. And it's part of my job as a parent to make sure you understand that."

"I understand that you need to do what's best for you. And I support your right to do that. If you're really not willing to call me from the office on nights you have to miss dinner, I may decide to make other dinner plans during the week so that I'm not in the position of waiting for you."

You can also use the Instant Influence process to encourage the other person to imagine the consequences for herself. When you get to Step 4 (Imagine you've changed. What would the positive outcomes be?), you might reframe it: Imagine you haven't changed. What would the outcomes be?

> "Suppose things keep going and your reports keep piling up. What do you imagine will happen next?"
> "Imagine that you keep forgetting to do your share of the chores. What do you think Dad and I will do next?"
> "If you keep coming home late and missing dinner without even calling me from the office, how do you see that affecting our relationship?"

The resistant person might respond in a way that puts the responsibility on you or someone else:

> "If I keep coming in late, Bailey will write me up and I'll get a bad report."
> "If I don't do my chores, I guess you and Dad will cut off my allowance for a while."
> "If I don't let you know when I'm not coming home, you'll probably be pretty hard to live with."

You might then reply in a way that puts the responsibility back on them:

> "That sounds accurate: you will have put yourself in a position to get a bad report."
> "Yes, you earn your allowance by doing chores. If you don't do chores, you won't get it for a while."
> "True. If you don't treat me with consideration, I probably won't be so happy with you."

The codeveloper of motivational interviewing, psychologist Bill Miller, referred to that as "letting the person stew in his own juices."[1] So even when you want to unleash consequences, you might find it more effective to let the other person be the one to bring them up, describe them, and evaluate what they mean to him.

Counterproductive Moves

The following approaches usually do not help move a resistant person to take positive action. In fact, they often have just the opposite effect:

- *Sarcasm.* If you're using autonomy-reinforcing statements like "It's up to you" or "This is your call to make" or "It's your choice," you might sound as if you're being sarcastic or dismissive. Be sure to speak in a sincere, genuine tone. It's all right to be distressed, concerned, or even angry, but not sarcastic.
- *Manipulation.* If you say something like "It's up to you to make the right decision" or "I know you'll do the correct thing," you're implying that you know what the right thing is and you're just waiting for the other person to catch up. This is the very opposite of reinforcing his autonomy. The more resistant the other person is, the more such statements are likely to backfire.
- *Giving advice or otherwise taking charge.* Resistance often means that the person is anxious about taking responsibility, so she's trying to put the responsibility on you. You'll say what you think should happen, and she'll resist it. From her point of view, problem solved! From your point of view, you're right back where you started. Don't take the bait. Use the Instant Influence process to keep responsibility for her actions squarely on her, where it belongs. Similarly, it's usually not helpful to tell someone she has to start taking responsibility.

SUCCESS STORY: A PIANO IS KEY

Lois had recently taken over a sales team at an electronics firm and had instituted a new system for tracking sales leads that she felt was working well. Only one team member—a man I'll call George—stubbornly refused to adopt the new procedure.

George had once had high sales numbers and a good record with the company, but even before Lois took over the department, his performance had started to slip. When Lois came on as department chief, he became even more recalcitrant. "If his numbers were up, I might let it slide," Lois told me. "But he's not pulling his weight, *and* he's not following the protocol that I know will help. I honestly think he could be a good salesman if he'd get with the program. But I've talked with him at least four times now! I hate to fire the guy—he just had his third kid, plus he's got a great severance package, so it would be very expensive for the company. But what am I supposed to do?"

Lois and I spoke about her options, and I asked her to send me an account of her progress. The following dialogue is based on what she sent:

GEORGE: I'm good at sales; I don't need to follow a system.

LOIS: Well, ultimately, it's up to you whether or not you use the new system. Everyone would like you to, but, technically, you don't have to. *[As we'd discussed, Lois was reinforcing George's autonomy. She knew she had to put extra effort into doing so because of how many conversations she'd already had in which she'd tried to force him to do things her way.]*

GEORGE: You mean I can get away with not using it? *[Can you hear the spark of motivation in this statement? George isn't saying, "I won't use it, then." He's acknowledging that he's supposed to use the new system and that he's trying to "get away" with something. By asking this question, he shows his awareness that his refusal may have consequences.]*

LOIS: No, eventually something may happen as a result, but it's still up to you to decide whether the potential consequences are meaningful enough for you to follow the system. *[Since George himself alluded to the potential consequences of his refusal,*

Lois is being up-front with him, while still reinforcing his autonomy.] You seem worried that there may be some negative repercussions from not using the system. What are your concerns? *[Instead of lecturing George or threatening him with consequences, Lois asks him to imagine what might happen.]*

GEORGE: Uh...I don't know. This is actually the first time I ever thought about it. What could happen? I'm so close to the pay raise. I wouldn't want that to be affected. *[Now that Lois is asking George questions and letting him express his concerns, he is beginning to think about what might happen rather than simply evading and resisting her.]*

LOIS: Well, George, let me just ask you, given that it's your choice, ultimately, what you do, if you did want to follow the system—I realize you've said you don't need to—but if you did want to follow it, why *might* you want to? *[Lois reinforces George's autonomy and moves into Step 1: Why might you change?]*

GEORGE: I already told you I'm not going to follow the system.

LOIS: Right now I'm not asking you whether you're going to do it or not. I know you don't like the system. But I'd still like to hear, *if* you were going to follow it, why you might do it. I'd be interested to hear your answer, just as a hypothetical. *[Keeping it hypothetical, emphasizing George's right to his own opinion, and asking for his thoughts rather than trying to win him over are all key here. Because George has been resistant, Lois must work extrahard to reinforce his autonomy, focusing on his choice and his thoughts.]*

GEORGE: Well, that's easy. If I were going to follow the system, I would do it to get you and everybody else off my back and to make sure I get the raise. *[George is at least theoretically considering a change here. Despite his repeated resistance, he is even offering two reasons for change.]*

LOIS: Sounds like there are at least two potential payoffs here. But tell me about everybody being "on your back"—that sounds hard. *[Lois is expressing empathy, which helps George feel heard. She's also asking an open-ended question, which might help to get him thinking.]*

GEORGE: It's really awful. It's like nobody remembers that a couple of years ago I was top salesman. Now they say things like, "There goes George again—breaking all the rules." It really would be nice if that could stop. Coming to work would be much nicer for me. *[This is all totally new information for Lois. She had no idea that people's opinions of George bothered him so much. She also sees how much it means to him that he was once top salesman.]*

LOIS: That really bothers you. I can see why you would want it to stop. Given that, why might you reconsider using at least some of the system? *[Because George is so resistant, Lois keeps returning to Step 1: Why might you change? At the same time, she's showing understanding of his concerns and continuing to reflect back any possible reason he might have for changing. Since they are now actually having a conversation, with George sharing his thoughts and feelings, Lois thinks that, for the first time, they might be able to communicate instead of just fight.]*

GEORGE: Because I guess there is *some* value in parts of it. *[Now George is focused less on external things—how Lois and the others would treat him—and more on the potential inherent value of the behavior itself. This is a promising sign. He is able to make this concession because Lois is not insisting that he think her way, thus leaving him room to appreciate at least some aspects of the new system.]*

LOIS: So George, on a scale of 1 to 10, where 1 means "not ready at all" and 10 means "completely ready," how ready are you to start following the system? *[Lois engages George in the process by using Step 2: How ready are you to change—on a scale from 1 to 10, where 1 means "not ready at all" and 10 means "totally ready"?]*

GEORGE: What kind of stupid question are you asking me? *[George is resisting this new approach. But he isn't refusing to answer.]*

LOIS: I just want to see where you're at with this. If you were going to rate your readiness, what number would you choose? *[With people who are resistant, you sometimes have to keep returning to the questions. You also benefit from phrasing each question in such a way as to allow maximum autonomy: "If you were going to rate your readiness, what number would you choose?"]*

GEORGE: I'd say 3, but who knows, that may change tomorrow. *[Notice how George is still protecting his autonomy by refusing to commit. Lois needs to acknowledge this and to respond by continuing to reinforce his autonomy.]*

LOIS: All right. Thank you. Can I ask another question? Why didn't you pick a lower number? *[Lois's "thank you" conveys appreciation for his response. George didn't have to answer her previous question. She then asks permission to continue.]*

GEORGE: Now you're really confusing me. You want me to be *less* motivated? *[As you can see, a resistant person often objects to every question, sometimes several times. You need a lot of patience and persistence to keep returning to the questions while reflecting back every tiny spark of motivation. Notice how George is now speaking in terms of what Lois wants rather than refusing to do what she's asking. Lois will seize this opening and reflect it back.]*

LOIS: George, I'm so glad you're concerned with what I want, but right now, I'm interested in what *you* want. You put your level of readiness to follow the system at a 3, and I'm curious. You could have picked a 2 or even a 1, and you didn't. So why did you pick a 3 and not a lower number? *[Like most people, George is surprised by this question and puzzled about why Lois is talking so much about what he wants. He's used to her talking about what she *wants*.]*

GEORGE: I really want that pay raise. *[George is continuing to identify his reasons for following the system, even though he has established that he does not want to follow it. If Lois were to ask him right now, "Will you follow the system?" George would say, "No!" But she isn't asking him that question. She's asking why he would follow it, if he did. So George has room to think positively about something that previously he has only been negative about.]*

LOIS: Okay, great. You might follow the system if you thought it would help you get the pay raise you want. *[Lois reflects back George's motivation in the most positive way possible, speaking in terms of what George wants and why, but never going beyond what George himself has said.]* Now, imagine that you have followed the system and gotten the pay raise. *[Lois links the behavior she wants with the outcome that George wants—a link that George himself has already made. Lois is not "bribing" George with a good consequence or threatening him with a bad one; she's just reinforcing what he's already told her. Which means she can now proceed to Step 4: Imagine you've changed. What would the positive outcomes be?]* Why would getting that pay raise be a good thing for you?

GEORGE [pausing for a long time to think]: I want to buy my daughter a piano. She's wanted one for several years now. *[For the first time, George is talking in a personal, heartfelt way about what he wants. A long silence often precedes this type of deeply personal statement, as it did with my father. And as I did with my dad, Lois had to work very hard not to jump in and help George fill the silence. His personal statement was her reward.]*

LOIS: So, following the system could increase the chance that you could buy the piano for your daughter. *[Again, Lois reflects George's motivation back to him. Remember: people change when they hear themselves say why they want to change. Notice how Lois also remembers to tie George's reason to the target behavior.]*

GEORGE: I guess you're right. I never made that connection. *[Asking George about his reasons has enabled him to make a new connection between what he wants and what Lois has been asking him to do.]*

LOIS: You could use your pay raise to buy your daughter a piano. *[Again, Lois is reflecting George's reason back to him, linking the behavior she wants with the outcome he wants. Notice how much reflection needs to be done with a person who begins by saying that he doesn't want to change.]* So tell me, why is it so important to you to finally get your daughter that piano? *[This is Lois's version of the "five whys." She may not ask why five times, but she is ready to dig a little deeper to help George delve into the most personal reasons he can find for wanting to change.]*

GEORGE: Because I never had one myself, and I always vowed to support the things my children were really interested in, especially the arts. *[George's responses are getting more and more personal. By getting in touch with his own reasons, he is becoming more invested in the change Lois is asking about. He is discovering his own motivations for making it.]*

LOIS: So, following the system, despite not liking every part of it, could allow you to do something you vowed to do a long time ago—to right a wrong of your own childhood. *[More reflection linking behavior and outcome.]*

GEORGE: Yes, I guess that would be good. I'd really like to do that for her. *[Lois senses that this is as far as George is ready to go at this point, since he seems very thoughtful and preoccupied with this new idea.]*

LOIS: So what's the next step, if any? *[Notice how this question, Step 6, keeps George's wishes at the center of the process, rather than imposing Lois's wishes on him.]*

GEORGE: Why don't I try the new system out for a week and see how it goes. Maybe there are some parts of it that would work for me. *[If George had not suggested this himself, Lois* might have picked the smallest possible change she could imagine, the way I asked my father if he could imagine giving up just two cigarettes per week. She might have asked him to try out one part of the new system for a week or even for a day. At this point, she is not trying for "full compliance" but simply attempting to get the process going. She needs to trust that it will take on a momentum of its own. If it doesn't, she can always do a second round of Instant Influence or impose the consequences and fire George. At least this way, though, she has a shot at motivating him.]

LOIS: George, that would be great! Would you be willing to meet with me again in a week so we can talk about how it's going?

GEORGE: Yeah, sure, whatever. You really love these little meetings, don't you? [As my father did, George is now reestablishing his autonomy by being a bit rude to Lois. But the important thing is that he has volunteered to try out the new system and has agreed to meet with her again. If he had said, "I don't see the need," Lois could have said something like, "Well, I would appreciate it if you would think about it, and we can revisit the idea of another meeting later on." To further reestablish his autonomy, George might now adopt the system so fully that Lois won't even need to meet with him. Or she may have to start the process again, asking George to use the system for a longer period of time. Either way, she has made more progress with him today than she ever has before.]

Tips for Working with Resistant People

• *Focus on the motivation, not the results.* I didn't care about my father cutting back by two measly cigarettes a week and coughing for "only" fifteen minutes every morning—I wanted him to give up smoking completely to protect his health. Lois didn't want George to make a couple of halfhearted changes and then get fired—she wanted him to adopt the system she believed in and bring his sales numbers up. It's tempting to go for big all-or-nothing results, but that is not how change happens. Pick the easiest possible change you can imagine, and trust that the first small step forward will lead to others.

• *Be willing to be surprised.* When my trainees talk to me about their most resistant colleagues, employees, or clients, they often insist, "A guy like that is *never* going to change." And they usually follow it up with, "And he'll never go along with these questions, either!" I most often reply, "You're basing those perceptions on all the past conversations you two have had. You've gotten to know each other's preferred ways of interacting, and, yes, they don't work. But this approach is new. He's never heard you talk this way before—and you have no idea how he'll answer when he does."

• *Periodically check your own motives.* Are you more interested in winning a power struggle than motivating your employee? Are you more committed to proving yourself right than inspiring your "stuck" colleague? Are you more excited about "not letting him get away with anything" than about creating a win-win with a potential client or business partner? If so, you probably won't have much success with Instant Influence, because you'll be seeking a goal that the method isn't designed for. Resistant people tend to provoke power struggles, so do your best to remain clear and committed to your true goals.

SUCCESS STORY: KEEPING THE DOOR OPEN

It can be disconcerting to get a 1 in response to Step 2: How ready are you to change—on a scale from 1 to 10, where 1 means "not ready at all" and 10 means "totally ready"? But with a little practice, you can become as comfortable with that answer as with any other.

Here's an instructive conversation based on an e-mail from one of my trainees, a sales supervisor at a pharmaceutical company. Andre is trying to motivate Leo to follow the sales system.

ANDRE: So, Leo, on a scale of 1 to 10, how ready are you to adopt the procedures we've worked out?

LEO: Honestly? I'm a 1. I can do it my way. I don't see why you don't just let me do it my way, like I've been doing for the past fifteen years. My numbers may not be the highest in our department, but they are very far from being the lowest.

ANDRE: How ready would you be to talk with me today to see what part of the system you might be able to integrate into your own method? Again, give me a number indicating your readiness, on a scale from 1 to 10. *[The first thing to do if the answer is a 1 is to ask for a smaller next-step change.]*

LEO: I'm still a 1, Andre. I don't see the point in talking about this, frankly. I don't think you could ever persuade me even if we talked all day.

ANDRE: All right. I hear you. What would it take for that 1 to grow into a 2? *[Once again, we're not looking for a big change. We're asking about the slightest conceivable change—from no motivation to the smallest possible amount.]*

LEO: Huh?

ANDRE: What would make you the slightest bit ready to discuss integrating a part of the system into your own sales approach? *[Always be ready to calmly reword any of the Instant Influence questions.]*

LEO: Well, uh…I guess if I thought you would really respect my disagreeing with some of the procedures. *[Leo tells Andre what he needs, a very good sign.]*

ANDRE: You've had many great ideas for our team over the years, and I always look forward to hearing your insightful comments. I will respect your thoughts and wishes about what will and won't work at this point in time. *[Andre is able to provide what Leo needs, but within parameters—"at this point in time." This leaves the door open for Andre to come back later, which he did. The second time around, Andre and Leo had a complete and very effective Instant Influence conversation. If*

*you can't influence someone to do what you think he should now,
try to get him to continue the conversation later.]*

Test Your Instant Influence Skills: Finding
the Spark of Motivation

A critical aspect of using Instant Influence with resistant people
is finding the tiny spark of motivation in an apparent refusal to
change and reflecting it back to them. See if you can find the
motivation in these examples of resistance, then write down
how you would respond if you were having the conversation.

- I'm not going to that program!
- I'm not going to follow *any* of the system!
- I can't hire a personal assistant until I am earning more
  money.
- I would exercise, but between the children, my job, and
  my mother's health problems, I really don't have the time.
- I don't need help for this—I can do it on my own.
- I'm not going to start turning in my reports until every-
  one in the office does it.
- I'd like to quit smoking, but I've tried more times than I
  care to remember. I just can't.
- I really can't afford to pay you overtime right now.
- My workload is already through the roof. I don't have
  time for another project.
- I try to come on time, but sometimes things just get in
  the way.

Possible responses:

I'm not going to that program! "I understand that you
wouldn't go to that program. But why might you go to some
other program?"

I'm not going to follow any of the system! "It seems very important to you to tell me how you feel about this. Why is it important to you that I understand your feelings about this?"

I can't hire a personal assistant until I am earning more money. "If you had all the money you needed, why might you want to hire an assistant?"

I would exercise, but between the children, my job, and my mother's health problems, I really don't have the time. "If you had all the time you needed, why might you want to exercise?"

I don't need help for this—I can do it on my own. "Why is this something you would want to do, with or without help?"

I'm not going to start turning in my reports until everyone in the office does it. "If everyone in the office were turning in their reports, why would you want to do it then?"

I'd like to quit smoking, but I've tried more times than I care to remember. I just can't. "Suppose quitting were easy and you knew for certain that you could do it. Why would you want to?"

I really can't afford to pay you overtime right now. "If money were no object, why might you want to pay me overtime?"

My workload is already through the roof. I don't have time for another project. "If you had all the time you needed, why might you want to take on this project?"

I try to come on time, but sometimes things just get in the way. "If you were completely in control of every factor, why might you want to come in on time?"

Resistant people can challenge us to the utmost. By the same token, a breakthrough with them can be sweeter than a dozen easier conversations. Using Instant Influence successfully with a resistant person doesn't just change the situation for the two of you. It can also renew your belief in our capacity to change.

CHAPTER SEVEN

Influencing Strangers

I nstant Influence works with virtually anyone, including strangers. My trainees and I have tried it with clerks, colleagues, neighbors, and service personnel. I have a patient who used it to get extra therapy sessions from her managed-care plan. Trainees have written to me about using Instant Influence to persuade store managers to accept returns after the date stipulated; to negotiate great prices with car salespeople; to help resolve conflicts over seat assignments on planes and trains and at ball games; to deal with hecklers at large business meetings and performances; to moderate panel discussions at conferences where the debate has gotten overheated; to get lower rates for home improvement work; to calm protesters who were objecting to the practices of a pharmaceutical company; and even to break up fights at football games. It's remarkable how many different ways Instant Influence can be used!

Of course, you might need to get creative when adapting the technique for different circumstances. In this chapter, I'll show you how to reach people in the situations that used to leave you screaming with frustration and now can be happily and quickly resolved to your satisfaction.

SUCCESS STORY: THE FRIENDLY SKIES

Luis is a probation officer I met in a training program. Criminal justice professionals often have less than fifteen minutes to spend with their probationers, so if they're going to move people to change, they need to work quickly. Skeptical at first, by the end of the program Luis was convinced that Instant Influence really works. He decided to try it during a phone conversation with Gladys, a customer service representative at an airline. He wanted to persuade her to honor some reward miles so he could get his two sons discounted tickets to Florida.

Gladys was about to transfer Luis to another department. He knew he didn't have much time and immediately plunged in:

LUIS: Gladys, wait, please...

GLADYS: What is it, Mr. Ortiz? I think maybe if I transfer you...

LUIS: Gladys, you can transfer me if you want to — I would rather you didn't — but before you do, can I ask you one question? *[Luis understands that if this process is to work, he must reinforce Gladys's autonomy, especially because she is in customer service and is probably used to being browbeaten and yelled at. So he asks her permission to have the conversation.]*

GLADYS: Sure. What is it?

LUIS: Well, you said that you want to help me. Why? *[Step 1: Why might you change?]*

GLADYS: Mr. Ortiz, my hands are tied here.

LUIS: Please. If you were to help me get the tickets using my reward miles, what would you get out of it? *[When dealing with strangers, it's especially important to be persistent. They have no personal incentive to engage in an Instant Influence conversation, so you often need to ask the same question several times in slightly different ways.]*

GLADYS: Please let me transfer you.

LUIS: If you must, I understand, but I would really appreciate your just answering my question first. *[This part of the conversation went on for a minute or so. Gladys kept trying to transfer Luis, and Luis kept trying to get her—always politely, always acknowledging that she didn't have to do it—to answer his question. Then, suddenly, the tone changed.]*

GLADYS: Mr. Ortiz, I don't know what to say.... I got into this career to help people; it's what I enjoy. Yes, I enjoy taking people's problems and seeing what I can do to help. It's what I have always been about. That's why I want to help you get these tickets. *[Now Gladys has offered a compelling, heartfelt reason for wanting to help Luis. Notice that when you use Instant Influence with strangers—or in any situation where you might have less time than usual in which to work—you may need to focus on only Step 1.]*

LUIS: I truly appreciate your answer. It sounds like you are passionate about your career and that it means a lot to you to help your customers. *[Now that Luis has heard some motivation, he can reflect it back to Gladys.]*

GLADYS *[almost sheepishly]:* Yes, Mr. Ortiz, it does mean a lot to me. I don't take it lightly. It's important to me. *[Because Luis has heard Gladys's motivation and reflected it back to her, she speaks even more intensely about what she wants: to help people.]*

LUIS: So, on a scale of 1 to 10...how important? *[Now that Gladys has answered the first question, Luis can move on to his slightly modified version of Step 2: How ready are you to change—on a scale from 1 to 10, where 1 means "not ready at all" and 10 means "totally ready"?]*

GLADYS: Maybe the most important. Maybe the reason I even do this job. *[Because Luis is dealing with a stranger, he doesn't insist on getting the number, although he might have done that. Instead, since Gladys has expressed a sincere desire to help him, Luis simply asks for more information.]*

LUIS: Why? *[As we've seen, this is the most powerful question in the Instant Influence arsenal. When your influence suggests any level of sincere motivation, simply ask, why?]*

GLADYS: Because I'm here to work hard, and I care about people, truly.

LUIS: So, one more question. *[This is Luis's way of continuing to ask permission. With strangers this is especially important. Customer service people, waitstaff, and other service workers frequently deal with customers who approach them with a sense of entitlement. Customers assume that they have to talk to them and do what they want. This reduces their autonomy and virtually guarantees resistance.]*

GLADYS *[welcoming, this time]*: Go ahead. *[Being asked permission makes Gladys feel respected and appreciated. When people feel this way, they often become more generous and helpful.]*

LUIS: What if you helped me get those two plane tickets today, for my sons. Why would that be good for you? *[Luis has jumped to Step 5: Why are those outcomes important to you?]*

GLADYS: It's obvious you're getting the raw end of this deal. You deserve these tickets; your sons deserve to go to Florida like you planned. I want to get these tickets for you. *[Notice how, even though Gladys doesn't answer Luis directly, she states her intention to help him. Imagine how defensive she might have been if Luis had said, "I'm getting the raw end of the deal! I deserve these tickets!" By focusing on what Gladys wants and on what would be good for her, Luis has tapped into her sincere wish to help him.]*

LUIS: So what might the next step be? *[Luis is correctly taking Gladys's heartfelt answer as agreement that something should be done. He's moved on to Step 6: What's the next step, if any? Again, by leaving the next step up to Gladys rather than telling her what he wants her to do, Luis has given Gladys room to take over the situation and to follow her own desire to help him.]*

The next thing Luis knew, Gladys had put him on hold. At first he thought it was all over. But then a supervisor came on the line. "I am not sure what you did to Gladys," the second woman said, "but I talked to her, and I want you to go ahead and book the tickets at the discounted price, and we will honor them with your reward points. Would that be okay?"

Luis thanked the supervisor and made sure to praise Gladys to the skies.

Behaviors, Not Attitudes

Focusing on positive, concrete behaviors is useful whenever we're using Instant Influence, but it's especially important when trying to reach strangers, particularly those you'll probably never see again. You can't expect a waiter to "change that attitude," but you might be able to move him or her to bring you a low-fat version of the daily special. You can't ask an airline clerk to "admit that company policy is unfair," but you can, as Luis did, encourage her to authorize your reward miles for discount tickets. Practice thinking of your objectives in terms of behaviors, not attitudes, and you'll have an easier time when you want to reach a stranger.

PREPARING TO INFLUENCE STRANGERS

Getting into the right frame of mind before using Instant Influence is particularly important with strangers. Here are some helpful points to keep in mind as you prepare yourself for the encounter.

• *No one expects you to use this approach.* Customer service people are used to being treated badly on the phone and in person. They don't expect their autonomy to be reinforced; often they don't even expect to be treated with respect or common courtesy. As a result, they may be defensive and sometimes critical, impatient, or rude. Many are expected to use prepared scripts and are monitored by others to make sure that they do. So, for you to get through to them—for your autonomy-reinforcing message to be heard and for your unusual questions to be answered—you'll need to be patient and persistent, as Luis was. Be prepared to repeat Step 1 (Why might you change?) at least half a dozen times. (For ideas about how to vary it, see later in the chapter.) Feeling gypped, losing your temper, and acting as if you are entitled to what you're asking for are perfectly natural reactions, but they will not help you make progress with Instant Influence.

• *You don't have the option of invoking consequences.* Occasionally, a company may worry about losing you as a customer, or a waiter may be concerned about not getting a tip. More often, you'll have to deal with people who are so far removed from your problem that ultimately they have only one reason to help you: because they want to. What a great opportunity to use Instant Influence! As Gladys proved to Luis, people often *do* want to help—and now you can encourage them to tap into that desire.

• *You may not realize how close you are to getting what you want.* For brevity's sake, I eliminated the part of Luis and Gladys's conversation in which they went round and round, with Gladys repeating that she had done everything she could, and Luis politely asking her why she *might* want to help him. When the breakthrough came, it was surprising and sudden. Certainly, Luis didn't expect it. You may not see it coming either. Try to remember that breakthroughs often seem to come out of the blue.

- *You need to detach from any sense of being in a power struggle and instead focus on getting what you want.* The person you're dealing with may never acknowledge your right to what you want—but he may, like Gladys, find a way to give it to you. His motivation for doing so, however, will probably not come from a sudden awareness of the correctness of your position. Rather, it will spring from discovering why he wants to help you even though he doesn't have to. If your goal is to prove to him that he does have to help you, you're setting yourself up for failure.

REINFORCING THE AUTONOMY OF STRANGERS

Instant Influence will work much better if you can foster a relationship with the person you're speaking to. Customer service people often work with a script or are rewarded for saving their company time and money. Your goal is to get this one particular customer service rep to start thinking about why she has a personal desire to help you.

If you want the rep to respond as an individual, however, you have to treat her as an individual. Venting frustrations about an incorrect credit charge or an inadequate product won't inspire her to help you. Your first objective is to reinforce her autonomy, as you would at the beginning of any Instant Influence conversation. Given how she is usually treated, you may have to work extra hard if you want her to hear—and believe—that you respect her.

Suppose you're upset about a late fee that you believe was incorrectly levied on your credit card. You might begin the conversation in one of these ways.

- *Acknowledge that she didn't cause the problem:* "Hey, it's not as if you personally added that fee to my card."

- *Acknowledge that she personally doesn't benefit from the problem:* "And it's not like that fee is going into *your* pocket."
- *Acknowledge that she, too, may be facing restrictions:* "I know you have rules to follow and people who monitor what you do."
- *Share your emotional state:* "I'm having a really hard time with this."
- *Apologize, if necessary, for your venting:* "I'm going to try not to take my frustration out on you, but please forgive me if I do."
- *Express appreciation:* "I'm so glad I reached you." Or, if she's said, "How can I help?" you might reply, "I'm so glad you can help me."

Having established that you respect her and are aware of her situation, you're now ready to offer a succinct explanation of your problem. Try to describe it as calmly and objectively as possible. Avoid expressing anger ("And then, in a totally unfair way, they added a late fee, which just makes me furious every time I think of it!"). Don't try to garner sympathy or to elicit any other type of emotional response. Just share the facts. If recounting them makes you so upset that you can't help expressing your frustration, acknowledge it briefly, apologizing if appropriate: "I'm sorry. I hope I'm not taking my frustration out on you, but I'm having a really hard time with this." Finally, reinforce her autonomy by making it clear that her choice of response is up to her: "I'm not sure if there's anything you can do about this." "Maybe there isn't anything you can do, but I hope you can." "I'm not trying to force you to do anything you can't do, but it would be great if you could…"

ADAPTING INSTANT INFLUENCE FOR USE
WITH STRANGERS

Be ready to skip steps of the process when using Instant Influence with strangers. In some situations — a neighborhood restaurant, a doctor's or dentist's office, or any local business — we might expect to develop a long-term relationship with the staff. In such a case, it might make sense to take more time with Instant Influence, but remember that clerks and support staff are often busy and will tend to want to limit the amount of time they spend with you. Still, if you know you'll be dealing with the same people again and again, it might be worth the effort to work through all six steps.

In other situations, including just about any phone call we make to customer service, we're dealing with people we'll likely never speak to again. We're not investing in a relationship but are simply trying to get as much of what we want as the situation allows. The faster Instant Influence works, the better — for our sake and theirs. Accordingly, we might focus on the first three steps, to tap into the reasons for change; and then the last step, which points us to action. We don't necessarily need to deepen commitment by using Steps 4 and 5.

In a pinch, simply focus on Steps 1 and 6:

"Why might you want to take the late charge off my credit card?"

"Okay, great. And what's our next step?"

Adapting Step 1

Part of me resists suggesting ways to vary Step 1, because it works so well as it is. If the original is the only version of Step 1 you ever use, even with strangers, you'll be a more effective motivator than if you were to use a tell-and-sell or a "high-threat" approach or simply lose your temper.

Sometimes, however, it is useful to have different ways to approach this question, especially if, like Luis, you find yourself having to repeat it several times before you finally get a welcoming response. Here are some variations you might want to try:

"Why might you decide to help me with this?"

"If this policy is completely inflexible, I understand. But you're on the phone with me now, so there must be somewhere we could go with this. Why is it important to you that we try to do something here?"

"There's an exception to every rule. So what would have to happen for you to make an exception here — and why would you want to make one?"

"Is there any chance you've ever done this in the past — and if you did, why did you do so?"

"Do you ever make exceptions? Someone must have made at least one exception before... If you've made an exception, why might you want to make one now?"

"I know things often get done differently, depending on circumstances. Can you think of any instances — maybe one in the past — when you might have wanted to help someone with a similar situation? Why might you have wanted to help him at that time?"

"We've been talking about some specific solutions. But can we take a break from that conversation for a moment? Can you suggest some other things that we haven't yet talked about that might work? Why might you want to help me do one of those?"

"What else could you do here? Why might you want to?"

Compromises and Bottom Lines

When you're trying to get a problem fixed and a customer service rep starts offering options, it's easy to get confused. You might think, *Oh, look, I did motivate her,* when in fact all she's doing is following a script, and nothing she's offering even comes close to what you want. In such a case, what should you do?

- If what she offers seems to be in the ballpark of what you're looking for, hear her out.
- If you're hearing a list of possibilities and none seems likely to work, politely interrupt, thank her, and reflect back what you've heard as positively as possible: "It sounds like you're trying to remedy the situation, and I appreciate it. It's not quite what I'm looking for, so let me ask you, why is it important for you to try to help me?"

Adapting Step 2

As you remember, Step 2 (How ready are you to change—on a scale from 1 to 10, where 1 means "not ready at all" and 10 means "totally ready"?) works best when both people know exactly what the number is supposed to measure. Are you asking your employee to be on time for the rest of the week, or for the rest of his life? Are you trying to motivate your father to quit smoking cold turkey, or to give up two cigarettes per week?

When you use Step 2 with strangers, it's good to have a realistic idea of the response you're likely to get and a clear sense of your bottom line. You can then use that minimum as the basis for your question: "Ideally, I'd like a full discount. But on a scale from 1 to 10, where 1 is 'not ready at all' and 10 is 'completely ready,' how ready are you to give me even half a discount?"

Often in these situations, what makes us happy is getting just a bit more than the person offered initially, even if it's not everything we wanted. Sometimes, of course, we don't have room for compromise and need to stick to our guns. But if compromise is possible, get clear about what you are willing to accept before putting Step 2 into words.

When you begin Step 2, you'll try to get the other person to give you an actual number. If they insist on describing their readiness in words, of course, you may need to let it go, though you can still ask, "Why not less ready?" instead of "Why not a lower number?" But ideally you'll persist, because the number offers a clarity and a precision that help you see exactly where the other person is in a way that the descriptions *completely ready to change* or *almost ready to change* just don't.

> "I know you're familiar with asking customers to rate how you've done, how good your services are. So, just so I understand more specifically how ready you are to help me, a number would be good."
>
> "Maybe it sounds mechanical, but if you don't mind..."
>
> "This would help me get a clear idea of how prepared you are to help me get this done..."

You may feel a bit silly following this formula with a stranger, especially with the first two or three strangers you try it on. Don't worry—the effectiveness of Instant Influence does not depend on how you feel.

What if your customer service rep says he's unwilling to answer this or any other question because he can't commit to doing what you ask? In that case, emphasize that you asked, "How *ready* would you be to do it," not "How likely are you to do it":

> "Suppose you did get the go-ahead from your supervisor? How ready would you be, on a scale of 1 to 10, to do what we're talking about?"

"Imagine that the final decision here was totally yours. On a scale of 1 to 10, how ready might you be to follow through?"

Generally, you want to help the rep switch out of "can versus can't" mode and into one where the key terms are *readiness* and *willingness*:

"I get that you can't do what I'm asking, but how ready would you be if you *could* do it?"

"You sound so helpful. I know you would help me if you could. So on a scale of 1 to 10, how willing would you say you are?"

Adapting Step 3

You should do your best to get the other person to answer Step 3 (Why didn't you pick a lower number?) rather than brush it off with a laugh, an evasion ("I don't really know how to answer that"), or a general answer ("It's my job"). The responses you get from strangers won't necessarily be as personal or as heart-felt as when you use Instant Influence with family, friends, and coworkers, but don't let that deter you from trying. As happened with Gladys, you just might get a genuine response about how much the influencee wants to help people or how deeply dedicated to her job she is.

With this step, I like to think that you are encouraging people to ponder. You're allowing them to pause and think about all the possible reasons they might have for doing something, then you're giving them the freedom to choose the one that's most appropriate. These activities—pondering and choosing—are rare in most customer service jobs, and many of these folks appreciate an opportunity to depart from prepared scripts and constant monitoring to simply think about what they want and why. They may not have a reason to want to help you, and they may choose not to help you even if they want to. But in my experience, people do enjoy helping others, as long as they're free to decide to do so. Therefore, suspend your disbelief, put your own reasons on the back burner, don't try to force anyone into anything, and see what happens.

If the person you're speaking with responds with a 1, then ask, "What would it take to make that 1 a 2?" As we learned earlier, this approach means that you're asking the other person to travel the shortest possible distance—from not willing to a tiny bit willing, which should make the transition easier to consider. Alternately, you could change what you're asking the person to do:

YOU: On a scale of 1 to 10, how willing would you be to give me a full discount?

CUSTOMER SERVICE: I would have to say, 1.

YOU: I'm sorry to hear that, but thank you for answering my question. What if I asked you to give me the partial discount you mentioned before, plus a reduction in the yearly fee? On a scale of 1 to 10, how willing might you be to do that?

Adapting Step 6

As I've mentioned, you can adapt Instant Influence for strangers by using Steps 1 to 3 and Step 6 (What's the next step, if any?) or by using Steps 1 and 6 only. Of course, if someone voluntarily offers you something you're willing to accept, you may be done; there may be no need for Step 6 at all. But I've found that reinforcing the other person's autonomy right until the end is more effective than switching into command mode. Which of the two options below do you think is more effective?

CUSTOMER SERVICE: The best I can offer you is to take off the late fee, but you'll have to pay the increased rate on the card.

You: Fine, do that then.

Customer Service: The best I can offer you is to take off the late fee, but you'll have to pay the increased rate on the card.

You: Okay, I appreciate your doing as much as you can. I know you wanted to help me as much as possible. So, what's our next step, if any?

With each approach, the outcome may be the same, though you may have a more pleasant interaction when using the second one. And it also might inspire the rep to say, "You know, there *is* one other thing I haven't tried" or "Even though I can't lower the rate, have you ever thought about switching your balance to a whole new card? I might be able to help you with that." Certainly, it costs you little to keep reinforcing the other person's autonomy and reflecting back her motivation. As long as you're having the conversation anyway, why not maximize your chances for success?

What you don't want is for the other person to "snap out of it" and realize that he has just gone the extra mile for you and that maybe there are some reasons that he didn't want to do that. So try to avoid such autonomy-negating statements as, "I'm glad you decided to do the right thing!" or "Finally, you're seeing it my way." Reflect back the other person's motivation and reinforce his autonomy until the moment you hang up. You might be pleasantly surprised at the results.

Test Your Instant Influence Skills: Influencing Strangers

This is a conversation you might have with a customer service representative from an airline. You had to cancel a flight due to a family crisis, and you were given a voucher for a replacement ticket that was good for up to one year. You're now trying to use that voucher one week past the expiration date. You begin with Step 1 (Why might you change?) and hope that you will be able to skip right to Step 6 (What's the next step, if any?) but, as often happens, you find that you have to keep reintroducing Step 1. In a notebook, write down some possible ways to rephrase Step 1 in response to every statement the clerk makes:

- I'm sorry, but our policy is to honor those vouchers for only one year, and you are now past the due date.
- I'm not authorized to extend the deadline for you.
- The company policy is very clear on this—I really don't have a choice.
- It won't help you to talk to a supervisor; he'll tell you the same thing I just did.
- I can offer you a 10 percent discount on your next flight, but that's the best I can do.

Possible responses:

I'm sorry, but our policy is to honor those vouchers for only one year, and you are now past the due date. "I completely understand that you are supposed to follow policy, and I realize you might not be able to help. But if you *were* able to help me work this out, why might you want to?"

I'm not authorized to extend the deadline for you. "Of course, you can only do what you're allowed to do. But if you *were* authorized to extend the deadline, why might you want to?"

The company policy is very clear on this—I really don't have a choice. "It sounds like you might like to help me if you did have a choice, and I really appreciate that. If you *could* help me, why would you want to?"

It won't help you to talk to a supervisor; he'll tell you the same thing I just did. "I understand there are lots of rules and regulations in place. But would you be willing to listen to a really dumb question? *If* you had the power to do what I'm asking—*if* you could help me—why might you want to?"

I can offer you a 10 percent discount on your next flight, but that's the best I can do. "It sounds like you're trying to remedy the situation, and I appreciate that. It's not quite what I'm looking for, so let me ask you this: Why is it important for you to try to help me?"

You've learned how to influence just about anyone: yourself, people who want to change, people who don't want to change, and strangers. Now it's time to learn how to evaluate your success, make an action plan, and cope when you don't get the result you wanted.

PART III

Making the Most of Your Results

CHAPTER EIGHT

Identifying Change

You've just invited a problematic employee into your office for an Instant Influence conversation. This man is great when he's on his own, but he's a disaster whenever he has to work as part of a team: he turns work in late, misses some team meetings, and sits in stony silence whenever he does show up. You're trying to inspire him to participate more fully, and he seems to be thinking hard about what you're saying. But he's still pretty quiet, and you don't know how to read his silence. Is he angry or just processing the conversation? What's your next move?

You're having an Instant Influence conversation with your extroverted and gregarious wife. You love her exuberant personality, but you're exhausted when you get home from work, and you'd really appreciate it if she'd agree to give you a full hour of silence every evening — no interruptions, no conversation, no demands. You're happy to chat with her at dinner, but you need some quiet time. And thanks to Instant Influence, you're finally able to show her why she might benefit from giving you a chance to unwind and recuperate from your day. So far, she hasn't given you an enthusiastic yes, but she's not stalking out of the room, either. What do you do now?

Your thirteen-year-old daughter, Julia, has been hanging out with Sonja, a fifteen-year-old girl you think is way too old for her. On their last trip to the mall, Sonja used her credit card to help your daughter buy some nonreturnable clothes, and now Julia owes her money. Today, Sonja invited your daughter to a boy-girl birthday party that you're sure Julia isn't ready for. You want Julia to agree to see Sonja only in school, and to your surprise, the Instant Influence conversation you've had with her didn't end in tears or confrontation. But you're not quite sure how things are progressing. How can you tell?

It's easy to proceed when Instant Influence goes well. You get to Step 6 (What's the next step, if any?), identify the next step, and make a formal or informal action plan. (We'll learn about action plans in chapter 9.) It's also clear what to do on the rare occasion when Instant Influence goes badly: ask permission to have the conversation again or simply reopen it at another time. (See chapter 10 to learn what to do when Instant Influence doesn't work.) But what about all those times in between, when you think you're getting through but can't be sure? What do you do then?

Your main goal is to keep the conversation moving in a positive direction while staying alert for any signs of progress. You do that in three ways:

1. Listen for "change talk."
2. Look for signs of change.
3. Troubleshoot any problem areas.

LISTEN FOR "CHANGE TALK"

"Change talk" is any statement uttered by the person you're talking to that suggests he is starting to think about change or perhaps even moving toward it.[1] It's what you listen for during the Instant Influence process and how you know that you're making progress. There are six types of change talk, each of which shows varying degrees of promise. From weakest (least likely to change) to strongest (most likely to change), they are ability talk, need talk, want talk, action talk, reasons talk, and commitment talk.

Ability Talk

"I can change." Ability talk is the weakest type of change talk because when people are speaking about ability, they're still thinking about how, and, as we've seen, it's far more beneficial to focus on why. Still, any interest in change is helpful, and ability talk gives you an opportunity to ask *why:*

EMPLOYEE: I know I could participate more in group meetings if I absolutely had to ...

YOU: But why might you want to participate? What would be in it for you?

Each type of change talk can vary in degree. The stronger the statement, the more likely you are to reach commitment talk—and, ultimately, to see the desired change itself. With ability talk, the spectrum looks like this:

Strongest: I'm positive I could participate more in meetings.
Moderate: I can participate more.
Weakest: I guess I could participate more.

Need Talk

"I need to change." Need talk is stronger than ability talk because it suggests a reason or a motive for change. Still, it's the second weakest type of change talk, because saying "I *need* to do something" usually suggests that there is an extrinsic reason at play. *Need* is often just another way of saying *should,* and anytime the word *should* is used, we risk triggering the law of psychological reactance. In most cases, people are far more likely to do what they want to do than anything that they need to do or should do. So, once again, try to move the influencee toward greater commitment by asking *why* and focusing on her wants:

WIFE: I do need to leave you alone for a while when you get home, don't I? I can see why you need some downtime.
YOU: I'm glad you get that—thank you. I really appreciate it. But can I ask you another question? Why might you *want* to give me that time?

Again, there's a spectrum of need talk that you might hear. The stronger the talk, the more likely the desired commitment talk will follow.

Strongest: I definitely need to give you some quiet time.
Moderate: I need to give you some quiet time.
Weakest: I probably need to give you some quiet time.

Want Talk

"I want to change." Now we're talking! Once someone expresses the desire to change, you're halfway home. Not all the way home, because, as we've seen, what really moves people to action is not simply acknowledging a desire to change but hearing themselves say *why* they want to change. So, once again, you can strengthen your influencee's commitment and move the process forward by asking *why:*

JULIA: Sonja can be kind of scary sometimes, but I really like her. I might want to see her only in school, like you said, but if she asks me to do something really cool, it's going to be hard for me to say no.

You: Honey, I'm glad to hear you want to keep Sonja as a school friend. But do you mind my asking why you might want to see her only in school? What do you think will be in it for you if you do?

Strongest: I absolutely want to see Sonja only in school.
Moderate: I want to see Sonja only in school.
Weakest: I might want to see Sonja only in school.

Action Talk

"I have already taken or am currently taking concrete action toward the target behavior/change." We are now at a somewhat higher level of change talk, and you can see why. When someone is telling you about an actual behavioral change, they're letting you know that they are already pretty motivated. Still, asking why can help move the person further.

EMPLOYEE: Actually, I've met every deadline so far for the team that I'm on now.

You: I'm so glad to hear it! Thank you for telling me about that. Here's something else I'd like to think about: Why do you think you've worked so hard to meet those deadlines? What have you gotten out of doing that?

Strongest: I've already met all the deadlines for my team.

Moderate: I've met some deadlines for my team.

Weakest: I guess I've been trying to do better meeting my deadlines, and I did meet one yesterday.

Reasons Talk

"I want/need to change because [some personal reason, such as] it will make me feel more satisfied with myself" *or* "I have taken steps to change because [some personal reason, such as] it gives me more free time for the things I enjoy most." Reasons talk is stronger than any of those we've covered thus far for two reasons. First, as we've seen, people change when they hear themselves say why they want to. Second, reasons talk incorporates elements from other types of change talk, such as want and need. Any reason will do, but the personal ("I'll feel better about myself") is usually better than the external ("I'll get more money"). If someone is giving you reasons talk, remember the "five whys." If you can, keep asking, "And why is that important?" until you hear a response that feels genuinely personal and heartfelt. The conversation can sometimes take a while, but the results you get from completing the process are definitely worth it, as the following dialogue illustrates:

WIFE: I want to give you that hour of quiet when you get home because you're going to be hell to live with if I don't!

YOU: Thanks. I'm glad to hear it. But can I ask, why is it important to you that I be easier to live with? *[first why]*

WIFE: Oh, come on. You're just a lot easier to be around when you're happier.

YOU: Why is it better for *you* when I'm happier? *[second why]*

WIFE: Really? You're serious? Okay, I actually kind of hate it when I sit there chatting to you and you're being polite but I can tell you're wishing I would stop. I'd be delighted to give

180

you an hour of quiet if it put you in a better frame of mind during dinner.

You: I'd like that, too. But what would be good for *you* about doing that? *[third why]*

Wife: Well, you wouldn't be so on edge, would you?

You: I'd sure try not to be. But why would *that* be important to you? *[fourth why]*

Wife: Then we could have a lot more fun at dinner. I miss the way we used to joke around. Lately, you're tired all the time, and you're so grouchy. Do you think we'd tease each other and just laugh more if you had that quiet hour?

You: I'd love it if we could. But why might that be good for *you* if we did? *[fifth why]*

Wife: I'd feel like you really *liked* me. I mean, I know you love me. But sometimes it feels like you don't like being with me—like you don't really like me very much.

You: Honey, I'm sorry. I had no idea. I'll try not to be that way. But you're telling me that you'd like to give me a quiet hour after work because then we'd have a great time during dinner and you'd see how much I really do like being with you.

Wife: Yes. That's exactly right.

You: So what's the next step, if any?

Wife [laughing]: Please, honey, do it for me! Take the time.

Strongest (taking steps *or* wanting to change *plus* an intrinsic motive): I really want to give you that quiet hour because then you'll be in a better mood at dinner and I'll be able to see how much you really do enjoy being with me.

Moderate (wanting to change *plus* extrinsic motive): I want you to have that quiet hour because in a good relationship, you try to do what the other person asks.

Weakest (needing to change *plus* extrinsic motive): I really need to give you that quiet hour because then maybe sometime you'll do something I ask you to do.

As you can see, the most important and strongest element in reasons talk is the personal, heartfelt, intrinsic motive. The next most important element is whether the person talks about taking steps (strongest), wanting to change (moderate), or needing to change (weakest). Someone who says he "needs to change" and gives a deeply personal, heartfelt reason is actually closer to making a commitment to change than is someone who says he's already taking steps to change but gives just an external reason. If you're hearing personal, heartfelt reasons in your reasons talk, you can probably move forward to make an action plan (see chapter 9).

Commitment Talk

"I will change." Finally, we're in the realm of commitment talk, the most important type of change talk and the ultimate goal of Instant Influence. Commitment talk includes a clear, future-oriented statement of the intention to do something specific. This is also the type of talk that research tells us is most strongly and consistently associated with change. However, for commitment talk to be truly effective, it needs to be accompanied by at least one personal reason:

> From now on, I'll participate in the team whenever I'm assigned to one. I'll show up at meetings prepared and ready to contribute. I want to participate fully because I'll feel so much better about myself if I make a real contribution.

> Okay, honey, I see your point. From now on, I'll give you an hour each day after work to just be by yourself and do whatever. But I'll expect you to be really ready to talk to me at dinner to make up for it! I'm so glad that we can

have fun at dinner again, so I know how much you like being with me.

I guess I'll just see Sonja at school then. She kind of scares me, so that feels right to me.

There is one circumstance, however, that trumps this whole system, and that is when someone shows genuine emotion. No matter how weak the rest of the conversation might seem, heart-felt feeling automatically makes it stronger. This goes for both negative emotion ("I'm so frustrated about this problem!") and positive emotion ("I'm so excited about where this could go!").

If you hear some negative emotion about a problem, reflect that back as well as a potential positive solution:

EMPLOYEE: I am so angry about what I'm like when there's a group involved! It's really hard for me to participate. I don't like that about myself. But it's true.

YOU: It sounds like this issue has made you really angry for a long time *[reflecting the emotion]*. And it also sounds like participating more fully might help free you from some of that anger *[reflecting the potential motivation]*. What do you think *[continuing to reinforce autonomy by returning the process back to the other person]*?

If you hear positive emotion, again, you can reflect both the emotion and the motivation.

WIFE: I really should give you that quiet hour because it would be so great if we could have more fun at dinner. When we were first dating, you made me laugh all the time. I miss that! I'd love to have that back again. Do you think we could?

You: I do think we could. And I hear how excited you are about giving me that quiet hour, so we could get that back *[reflecting the reasons why your wife wants to do something, even though she used the word* should*].*

Once you realize how important emotion can be, you'll listen for it more carefully and reflect it back more enthusiastically. Your reflection will reinforce the emotion and thus the desire to change.

Remember, there are two types of talk that signal readiness for an action plan: commitment talk accompanied by at least one personal reason for change, and any reason for change that is expressed with strong emotion. All other types of talk are hopeful signs of progress, and you should be encouraging, in your first Instant Influence conversation and beyond. But only proceed to an action plan when you hear commitment talk with at least one intrinsic reason, *or* reason talk plus strong emotion.

Test Your Instant Influence Skills:
Recognizing Readiness

Read the following statements. Check each statement that you believe signals a readiness to change, then determine why by classifying the type of change talk. Write down your explanation in a notebook.

- ☐ I'm just so sick of being tired in school every day! I really need to get to bed earlier. I can't stand what keeps happening when I don't!
- ☐ I know I could make some time each week to call Mom and Aunt Jane. I never talk to them at all anymore.
- ☐ I really want to get to the gym more often.

☐ I'm going to read at least one new book in my field every month. It won't be easy, but I need to feel like I'm still growing. Otherwise, I just feel old, and I hate that.

☐ I want to spend more time with my kids. Maybe if we did a weekly pizza run, that might work.

☐ My finances are such a mess; I'm embarrassed to talk about it. I've got to do something about them soon.

☐ I've already started putting something away for retirement, but I'm going to increase my monthly contribution starting this month and talk to a financial adviser next month. If I don't, I'm looking at a pretty bleak old age.

☐ I've gotten *some* work done on my quarterly reports, but the new ones will be due before the old ones.

☐ I'd like to ask my boss to consider me for a promotion. When I think about who's gotten recognition in my company instead of me, it just makes my blood boil.

☐ I'm so excited about this new nutritionist I've found. I'd like to follow her diet to the letter. I can't wait to see what great results I'll get.

Answers:

I'm just so sick of being tired in school every day! I really need to get to bed earlier. I can't stand what keeps happening when I don't! Strong emotion; more likely to produce change.

I know I could make some time each week to call Mom and Aunt Jane. I never talk to them at all anymore. Ability talk ("I could..."); less likely to produce change.

I really want to get to the gym more often. Want talk ("I really want to..."); less likely to produce change.

I'm going to read at least one new book in my field every month. It won't be easy, but I need to feel like I'm still growing. Otherwise, I just feel old, and I hate that. Commitment talk with reasons ("I'm going to..."); more likely to produce change.

I want to spend more time with my kids. Maybe if we did a

weekly pizza run, that might work. Want talk ("I want to..."); less likely to produce change.

My finances are such a mess; I'm embarrassed to talk about it. I've got to do something about them soon. Need talk ("I've got to..."); less likely to produce change.

I've already started putting something away for retirement, but I'm going to increase my monthly contribution starting this month and talk to a financial adviser next month. If I don't, I'm looking at a pretty bleak old age. Commitment talk with reasons ("I'm going to..."); more likely to produce change.

I've gotten some work done on my quarterly reports, but the new ones will be due before the old ones. Action talk ("I've gotten some work done..."); more likely to produce change.

I'd like to ask my boss to consider me for a promotion. When I think about who's gotten recognition in my company instead of me, it just makes my blood boil. Strong emotion; more likely to produce change.

I'm so excited about this new nutritionist I've found. I'd like to follow her diet to the letter. I can't wait to see what great results I'll get. Strong emotion; more likely to produce change.

LOOK FOR SIGNS OF CHANGE

Sometimes you can detect change in the language people use. Other times you must listen for signs of change in their tone of voice or in the emotions they express. Here are some nonverbal and indirect cues that might indicate the wheels of change are turning:

• *Pauses, becoming quiet, or speaking in fits and starts.* When the conversation halts or slows down, that means the other person is thinking hard about the change that is being proposed. Ideally, you should remain silent and wait—avoid filling in any silences—but if you must say something, use one of the autonomy-reinforcing statements from chapter 2.

• *More resistance than before.* Paradoxically, renewed resistance may indicate that change is being considered; your influencee is responding with frustration. Once again, try not to say anything. It's the other person's process, and she's working it out—let her. If you really feel the need to say something, you might acknowledge her resistance by noting its connection to change: "Sometimes people do get angry when change is on the horizon" or "Even good changes can be uncomfortable, since they mean a break in our regular routine." Often, people will shift ground again, responding to these statements by defending their desire, readiness, or willingness to change.

• *Confusion.* If you get a flurry of questions and concerns ("What about this?" "I don't understand that." "I'm confused about this other thing.") or if you're hit with a series of non sequiturs or inconclusive statements, you're seeing a response to change. It's just taking the other person a little while to process everything. Again, silence is best. If you must respond to the questions, you might reassure the other person that the two of you will get to them in time; now you're just focusing on the reasons why she might want to change.

• *Sarcasm.* This means you're being tested, particularly if the sarcasm takes the form of putting responsibility back on you ("You're the expert, aren't you?" "Why don't you just *tell* me what to do!" "Just hand me the script you'd like me to follow and I'll cater to your every whim, okay?"). You've respected the other person's autonomy, and he's begun to respond accordingly, but first he's checking to make sure you really mean it (though he might not be aware that's what he's doing). Just sit tight if you can. Try not to respond. But if you feel you must say something, you'll want to be prepared. Familiarize yourself with the list of possible responses later in this chapter.

- *Gently shifting responsibility back to you.* "What do you think I should do now?" "If you were me, how would you handle this?" As when sarcasm is used, this sort of response is meant to test you. Don't take the bait. Remain silent if possible. Use one of the responses provided later in the chapter if you feel you must say something.

- *Questions.* "You think that's easy?" "How am I supposed to do that?" "I can't do that. Why do you think I can?" "Why should I?" However hostile these questions might seem initially, they really are opportunities. Ideally, you will remain silent. If you feel you must say something, consider using one of the responses provided later in the chapter.

- *Reductions in resistance.* "Yeah, I guess I could do that..." "You probably have a point there." "I can kind of see what you mean." These are all openings that should encourage you tremendously. If resistance is declining, then motivation may be flooding in or, at the very least, some barriers may be crashing down. Remember, *anything* is better than an outright no. If you ask about the possibility of, say, using a sales procedure, and the employee says "Probably not," notice that there is an opening there, tiny though it may be. You now have the green light to respond, "Without yet thinking about how likely you are to do it, why *might* you do it?"

- *Imagining change.* "It would be great if..." "If only..." Sometimes these words convey pure excitement about the prospect of change. Other times the person's tone may reveal that she feels she can't do it and doesn't believe in it. Instead of genuinely wondering about the possibility, she's dismissing it. In that case, motivate her further by asking, "*What* would be great about it?"

- *Excuses.* "I can't because..." "It won't work since..." Again, as hard as it is to believe, such excuses are good news. Giving reasons for not doing something is one of the strongest signs that a person is seriously considering doing it. And because she is considering it, she is arguing against it. Don't fall into the trap of affirming her negative reasons or of suggesting that these excuses are just a way for her to dodge responsibility. Instead ask, "But why would you do it, if that reason not to didn't exist?" or "If you could wave a magic wand and make that problem disappear, then why would you do it?"

• *Legitimate reasons.* As counterintuitive as it seems, treat legitimate reasons for not doing something the same way you would excuses, and never suggest to the other person that you think he's avoiding responsibility. The point is not whether his reasons are good but rather to get his focus on the question *why.* So ask him to wave a magic wand and make the reasons go away, and then to think about why he *wants to* rather than why he can't do it.

Any sign of change means that you're making progress. Whether you see that progress in your first Instant Influence conversation or at a later time doesn't really matter. The process of change has begun!

If You're Being Tested...

If you are faced with a sarcastic remark or a polite effort to return the decision-making responsibility to you, remain silent if you can. If you can't, here are some possible responses:

• I honestly don't know what you should do.
• I have no idea what I'd do in your place.
• I could think about what I might do, at some point, and let you know...but for now, I'm more interested in hearing about why *you* might want to do this thing we're talking about, since it really is up to you.
• Yes, I *am* the boss [or the parent, or some other type of authority figure], and I do know what I want you to do, but now we're talking about what *you* want. We can switch gears if you want to, but I

really think that things will work best if we can get in sync and align our wants in some way.

- It sounds like you really want to get going on this problem. Why is it so important to you?

TROUBLESHOOT ANY PROBLEM AREAS

Usually, the Instant Influence process goes smoothly. But every so often people balk, resist, or just slow down. Here are some ideas for responses that will keep the conversation moving forward in a productive and positive direction when someone:

- *interrupts:* "For now, I'm more interested in focusing on the positive, and I'd appreciate it if you'd be willing to answer a different question: Why might you want to do this?

- *raises legitimate objections:* "Okay, we'll talk about that, but right now, I want to know why you might want to do this."

"I agree. We'll talk about that, but right now, I want to know why..."

"I'm so sorry. We'll talk about that, but right now, I want to know why..."

"At this moment I don't agree, but I'd love to hear more of your concerns. Right now, though, I'd like to know why..."

- *cuts off the whole conversation:* "I'm not interested in making you talk, but would it be okay if we talked about this again—and you pick the time?" [We all know there are consequences for not doing something, so you don't need to bring them into this part of the conversation, especially since consequences do little to motivate change.]

- *seems frustrated with the process or is simply ready to end it:* Move on to the next step or go directly to Step 6 (What's the next step, if any?): "So what's the next step, if any?"

"What would you like to do about this next...if anything?"

"What would you like to see happen next, and how do you want to be a part of that?"

Alternatively, to put the process on hold temporarily: "Thank you for talking with me. Would you mind if we talked about this again sometime? Would you be willing to pick a time?"

Signs of Impatience

The Instant Influence process is designed to work in seven minutes, so, in theory, the conversation should be over before anyone has time to be impatient. If it runs a bit longer, however, or if you're dealing with a very resistant person, you may notice some signs of frustration: "How much longer is this going to take?"; "I don't know..." (especially when said repeatedly in response to different questions); sighs and yawns; lack of eye contact and other types of guarded body language, including crossed arms, leaning back in a chair, angry or wary glaring. If you run into a roadblock with Instant Influence, always reflect back the other person's resistance so that you are reinforcing his autonomy and returning the responsibility to him:

"You seem frustrated talking about this. We don't have to talk about it now, but would you be willing to talk about it at another time of your choosing?"

"I can see you're distracted. Why might you want to continue talking about this even so?"

Or simply jump ahead to Step 6:

"I'm getting the impression that you want to stop now. So what's the next step, if any?"

In most cases, your Instant Influence conversations will lead to change. What's the best way to guarantee that action is taken? In chapter 9, we'll explore the most effective ways to make action plans that ensure concrete and lasting change.

CHAPTER NINE

Making an Action Plan

Once you've heard commitment talk plus reasons, or reasons for change expressed with strong emotion, your influencee is ready to make an action plan. An action plan is a personal contract, written or oral, that lays out exactly what actions the influencee commits to. Because it is a personal contract, there is no second party. It's a plan that makes the influencee accountable to herself. She becomes the enforcer of her own contract. You can make an action plan when you use the Instant Influence process yourself, or you can encourage your influencee (your employee, child, friend, or spouse) to make one, possibly with your help.

The person creating the action plan decides what form, written or oral, formal or informal, it will take. Ideally, it will include the following elements:

• *A clear behavioral goal, something specific and measurable.* For example, "Reply to every e-mail I receive this week within twenty-four hours." "Do my chores every day for a week without being reminded." "For the next two weeks, call each time I'm going to be late getting home from work."

• *A description of just one step—the next step—in the process.* If action doesn't continue in the right direction, you can have another Instant Influence conversation and make another action plan, but for now, stick to just one step. As we've seen, people are often willing to do something small and simple when larger changes seem daunting. And remember, if someone picks a small step, that doesn't mean he won't do more. People sometimes play it safe and commit to a little, even when they plan to do more. Or, after doing a little and having experienced an actual benefit, they may then decide to do more.

• *A time frame.* You're looking at the short term—ideally somewhere from one to thirty day(s)—so the plan seems doable.

• *A method.* How will you achieve your goal? "I'll put aside the first fifteen minutes each day to answer the previous day's e-mails." "I'll post all my chores on my bulletin board and check them off each day after I've done them." "I'll set the alarm on my phone for 5 p.m. as a reminder to call home." Naming a method makes the action seem possible and therefore more likely to get done.

• *At least one but ideally two or three reasons for the action.* The more heartfelt and personal the reasons, the more powerful the action plan will be. (Use the "five whys" to help your influencee identify deeply felt reasons.)

• *A description of potential obstacles and an explanation of how they will be overcome.* Optional.

• *A description of what help the person expects or plans to get from someone else.* Optional.

• *A backup plan or a statement of commitment to create a backup plan if the initial plan does not work.* Optional.

If an action plan is written, it can be signed and dated to solidify the commitment. It also might be helpful to give a copy to someone else—a friend, counselor, spouse, or colleague—since making a commitment public often motivates us to keep it. Work-based action plans can serve another purpose as well: documentation of a conversation with an employer or supervisor, so both parties have a record of what was agreed to during the meeting.

Remember, however, that an action plan is a *personal* contract. If it starts to feel like a promise to someone else, especially an authority figure, then any benefit from the Instant Influence process will be lost. The influencee needs to know that she's changing because she wants to, and not for any other reason. So if you're creating an action plan for yourself or helping someone else make one, think carefully about whether anyone else should see it. Maintaining an influencee's autonomy is critical. That's also why the person making the action plan decides whether the plan should be oral or written. Sometimes an influencer would prefer a written plan, but, ideally, he'll let his preferences take a backseat to the wishes of the influencee, thereby reinforcing her autonomy.

When *Not* to Make an Action Plan

As we saw in chapter 8, there are two types of change talk that should prompt an action plan: commitment talk that is accompanied by strong heartfelt reasons, and any reason expressed with strong emotion. If you haven't heard either of those yet, it's not time to make an action plan. In fact, making an action plan prematurely can do more harm than good. The science on this point is very clear: creating an action plan with someone who is not yet ready to act makes whatever motivation you've accessed disappear.[1]

What do you do instead? Simply leave the door open by saying something like, "I'll be curious to see what you might decide on this, if anything." The other person will get there in his own time, and when he does, he'll be operating from a strong, heartfelt commitment, which will move him further than threats, enticements, or consequences ever could.

HOW FORMAL SHOULD AN ACTION PLAN BE?

My trainees often ask whether they need a formal, written action plan, or whether it's enough to simply clarify a specific commitment. Because each situation is unique, it depends. Take your cue from the person you are trying to influence. Your first consideration should be maintaining and reinforcing that person's autonomy. If making a formal action plan will interfere with that goal, don't do it. If a formal plan will make the influencee feel more responsible and empowered, go right ahead.

Of course, some people are accustomed to formal action plans. The corporate leaders at GE, for example, routinely draft "commitment letters" to memorialize their latest plans. Business and executive coaches almost always work with their clients to develop written plans, as do many people in psychotherapy, social work, criminal justice, and the medical field.[2] Some teachers even ask their students to devise their own assignments.[3] Lots of people will find it reasonable and routine to draft and perhaps share an action plan.

But what if you work with people who aren't used to this sort of approach? Once, for instance, I helped some execs at a boating company who wanted to motivate the dockside supervisor of their boat-rental outlet. When they asked the man to write out his action plan, he said angrily, "I don't write *anything*. Why would I write this?" Having him write a plan made no sense. However, if an executive asked permission to take notes and to write an action plan for him, that might have worked. Reviewing the plan together, revising it, and then signing and dating it as a "team" might have put some extra oomph behind the agreed-on change.

Decades of research has shown that written plans, especially those written by the person who is going to take action, are much more effective than oral contracts. Still, as I've stressed throughout this book, reinforcing autonomy trumps pretty much everything else. Tell the person you're working with that any decisions about the action plan are up to him—and don't waver.

If you do opt for an oral action plan, make sure it includes what will be done, when it will be done, how it will be done, and why.

SUCCESS STORY: A REAL REASON TO CHANGE

Dana is a nurse I'd trained to use Instant Influence with ER patients. She had been frustrated for months by her apparent inability to get started on a healthful eating plan and decided to try my technique on herself.

Like many people, Dana expected that her deep-seated reasons for weight loss would have to do with looking better, feeling better, and being able to wear more fashionable clothes. What she discovered, however, was far different. She sent me the following e-mail:

Why did I want to lose weight? It's weird. I never would have expected it. But the image that kept coming to mind was my aunt Sylvia. She was my favorite aunt, always ready for a good time, always out and about. Her husband died when I was about eight, and I remember this long string of boyfriends who were always taking her dancing and on these romantic holidays, to the Caribbean and back to Puerto Rico, and all sorts of places. But she was also about fifty or sixty pounds overweight, and she died of a heart attack when I was sixteen.

She always seemed so happy and full of life. I hated that she died so young. I wanted her to give me advice on men, and she did, a little, when I was a teenager, but then she was gone.

Well, I have a niece I dearly love, and now she's eight years old, too. When I got to Step 5 [Why are those outcomes important to you?], I kept thinking, what if I'm not around when Isabel starts having boyfriends? What if there's stuff she can't talk to her mom about, and I'm just not there to help her?

It sounds weird, I know. But that's what got to me. It must have, because I've been on my eating plan for two months now, and so far, I'm doing OK. And whenever I feel like "breaking the rules," I just think of Isabel turning fifteen, sixteen, seventeen, and I guess that helps, because so far, I've been pretty good about staying on course!

I wrote back and asked Dana if she'd be willing to send me a copy of her action plan so that I could use it for this book. Here's what she sent:

I, Dana, promise myself to keep to my healthy eating plan for three months, starting tomorrow. I promise that if I slip and "fall off" the plan, I will start up again *the very next meal.* I will stick to my plan by: (1) planning my meals and snacks one week at a time; (2) shopping on Sunday evenings and making up weekly lunches and snack packs; (3) posting my weekly meal plan on the fridge. I will do this because I want to lose weight (30 pounds). I want to lose weight because I want to live a long and healthy life and be around when my niece is a teenager, so I can give her advice about guys!!!!
Signed,
Dana
February 18, 2010

> **FAQs About Action Plans**
>
> - *How do you decide when to negotiate an action plan?* When you hear some clear commitment talk plus at least one intrinsic reason for change, or reason talk accompanied by strong emotion, from whoever is going to take action. (For more on commitment talk, see chapter 8.)
> - *What if someone agrees to an action plan but picks a behavior that's too easy or a step that's too small?* Ask why he might agree to do a bit more.
> - *What if someone agrees to an action plan, but picks a behavior that's too difficult or a step that's too big?* Ask why she might agree to do a bit less.

MOVING FROM *WHY* TO *HOW*

Once we're ready to make an action plan, our focus shifts a bit. We've been interested in the why, but now we need to focus on the how.

Take another look at Dana's action plan. Notice that she doesn't just state her goal (to stick to her eating plan for three months); she says how she expects to achieve it (planning meals in advance; shopping and preparing food ahead of time; posting menus on the refrigerator). These specifics help in three important ways:

1. They give her less to think about when she is actually carrying out her plan. All of her decisions have already been made: how she'll shop, when she'll cook, how often she'll prepare food for the week. With all of that out of the way, she has more energy to focus on the action itself.

2. They make it clear to Dana that she is serious. This isn't some vague idea; this is something she has thought through.

198

The specific elements of her action plan reinforce Dana's sense that she is committed, that she really wants this change, and that she is going to make it happen.

3. *They make the change easier to visualize, and therefore easier to attain.* Often, when we have been stuck in a pattern for a long time, we find it hard to imagine that we can do things any other way. One of the most difficult aspects of beating an addiction, for example, is breaking the routines and habits associated with the addictive behavior: "When my friends and I get together, we go to the bar and have a few drinks." "After dinner, I always sit on the couch and smoke a cigarette." People who are trying to overcome addictions are advised to change their routines: go to the movies instead of to the bar, perhaps with different friends; sit in an easy chair rather than on the couch after dinner, or maybe go outside for a walk. Trying to establish any new behavior involves changing lots of little details. If Dana can visualize some of the details in her new routine—if she can imagine herself shopping and preparing food on Sunday evening; if she can picture that new meal plan posted on her fridge—she can begin to accept and therefore act on the change she has committed to.

Sometimes figuring out the how can be challenging, and often we need help, either in the form of technical information ("I'd like to start looking for a new job, but I'm not happy with the way I present myself in my résumé") or moral support ("I'd like to stop procrastinating, but somehow I always seem to end up on the couch watching TV instead of doing what I've planned"). If you're working on a change of your own, you might want to go to friends, experts, or other sources for information, advice, or moral support. If you're supporting someone else's change, now may be the time to offer the help and advice that you've resisted giving throughout this process.

Remember, you always want to reinforce the other person's

autonomy. In that spirit, you would do well to let him have the first crack at explaining how:

EMPLOYEE: I'm going to use the new performance review procedure every time I call someone in for the rest of the week, because I want to be the most effective team leader I can. Leadership is really important to me, and I see that if I'm breaking the rules, I'm letting my team down.

YOU: Great. I hear that you're planning to use the procedure for the coming week and that you've got some very strong reasons for doing so. Can I ask for some detail about how you plan to make sure this happens? How are you going to help yourself meet the goal you've laid out?

EMPLOYEE: Um...I don't know. I'll just do it. You don't have to worry.

YOU: I'm not worried. But I am curious. You've been using a different procedure for quite a while, and I can imagine it might be easy to forget to use this one. Do you plan to do anything to remind yourself about the new procedure?

EMPLOYEE: I hadn't thought of it, but that might be a good idea. I guess I could keep a copy of the new procedure on my desk while I'm talking to people. I won't need to read the script, but seeing it will remind me that I have to use it.

YOU: Sounds good. I know with me, my desk can get cluttered and I can miss things. Do you think maybe a Post-it on the phone might also be a good idea?

As you can see, the focus is always on helping the other person do what he's already said he wants to do, for his own reasons. You can absolutely offer your assistance and advice, but be careful not to take over the process. Also, try to keep an open mind. Sometimes people need to reject our solutions to preserve their own autonomy ("A Post-it on the phone isn't going to work for me"); other times they can come up with solutions we never would have thought of that work much better ("but I am going to keep a scorecard on my desk and rate myself after each meeting, so I'm sure I'm using the procedure in the best way possible").

I know how easy it is to fall into the role of the person with all the answers. But I've also seen, time and again, that giving up that authority and genuinely investing in the other person's autonomy can have enormous dividends, as he reveals himself to be a more independent, self-confident, and creative person than we ever might have dreamed.

CRAFTING YOUR OWN ACTION PLAN

Suppose you're creating an action plan for yourself. How do you begin?

1. Zero in on a small, specific, and doable first step. Make sure that you're following the Dead Man's Rule. Don't target a behavior ("I won't put things off") that a dead man could do as well. Avoid vague statements about attitude ("I'll have a more positive outlook") or results ("I'll improve my relationship with my kids"). Use positive, specific language to identify a measurable, observable step, something that is entirely within your control. Pick the *next* step in the process — not "I'll spend more time with my family," but "I'll play a board game with my family this week and order in pizza with them afterward."

2. Decide when that step will be completed. A quick turnaround time is usually best, but also consider attaching the target behavior to something that is already a routine: paying bills, taking a shower, a weekly staff meeting, a coffee break. Cognitive scientists Peter Gollwitzer and V. Brandstaetter found that students were more likely to complete assignments when they stated exactly when they would work on them and when they tied their completion to already-established routines.[4]

3. Identify the strategies—how *the step will be done.* This is often tricky because people who have gotten to this point sometimes don't like thinking about the details. Change can provoke anxiety, and imagining how you'll do something that you haven't previously been willing or able to do can make you want to push the whole question away. So go easy on the strategies in order to maintain the progress you've achieved.

HELPING SOMEONE ELSE CRAFT AN ACTION PLAN

Perhaps you know someone (a loved one, a colleague, or an employee) who is excited about creating her own action plan. Share with her what you learned when creating your action plan (see the previous section) and follow these guidelines as well:

1. Pick a manageable step. Encourage the other person to shoot for a somewhat smaller step than what she may first suggest. But keep in mind what organizational psychologists Edwin Locke and Gary Latham found in a landmark study: when workers set their own goals, they set goals that were harder to achieve than the ones supervisors assigned to them—and they were more likely to achieve those goals.[5] You don't have to totally rein in your influencee, but you do want to help her experience success. Picking a somewhat easier goal, rather than a harder one, can help her do just that. It's more important to increase an influencee's chances of success than for her to change quickly.

2. Focus on how the change will be made. If the other person says, "I don't know how I'm going to do it—I'll just do it!" try one or more of the following responses:

202

"I believe you, but it can be helpful to identify how. Would you be willing to think for a minute about which strategies you might use?"

"I want to make sure you have all the help and resources you need to get this done. If I hear your thoughts on strategies, we might come up with some ways to get you the resources or training you need. Would you be willing to brainstorm with me here?"

"Why might you want to think more specifically about some strategies?"

3. Return to the question of why the person wants to take this step. At this point, you're working as a "framer," helping to restate any reasons as positively as you can. Help steer the influencee away from less desirable negative framing and toward more desirable positive framing:

Less desirable: "I want to stop being late because being late makes me feel anxious and tense and I end up feeling incompetent and selfish" *[reason not to do something to avoid a negative outcome].*

More desirable: "I want to come in on time because I'll feel more relaxed and on top of things, and I'll feel like a more competent and helpful person" *[reason to do something for a positive outcome].*

Many of us are used to framing things in a negative light, focusing on all the dire consequences of not doing what we think should be done, but there's a lot of research that supports the power of positive framing. As we learned in chapter 3, people who give positive reasons to quit smoking ("If I stop smoking, my clothes will smell better, my family will spend more time with me, and that will make me feel good") are nearly three times more likely to stay away from cigarettes for six weeks than are people who give negative reasons ("If I don't stop smoking, I may get cancer, my clothes will continue to smell, and my family will spend less and less time with me because of the secondhand smoke").

If your Instant Influence conversation took place in a work setting and you feel the need to take notes as your influencee launches into his action plan, ask his permission before doing so. This subtly reinforces his autonomy and ownership of the process. If you were to begin taking notes without asking permission first, you'd give a nonverbal message indicating that you will be monitoring his compliance and that you are in control.

Test Your Instant Influence Skills: Positive Framing

You're working with a sales agent who is creating an action plan: she has agreed to use the company sales procedure for all her calls for the next three weeks. You have asked her to reiterate why she wants to use the procedure, which she did in the list below. Read each statement, and on a separate sheet of paper write down how you would reflect the statement back to her. If she is making a positive statement, echo it. If her statement is negative, reframe it as a positive one. If it is mixed, keep the positive and reframe the negative portion. Then keep reading for some possible solutions.

- If I don't use the new procedure, I'm pretty sure my sales will fall off.
- Using the new procedure will enable me to earn enough money to pay off my credit cards. I'm so sick of being in debt!
- Sticking with my old way is going to lead to trouble — some of my coworkers are already mad at me, and I hate that.

- I like being one of the group, and everyone else is on board with this. I don't like being left out.
- If everyone else thinks this is a good idea, I owe it to myself to at least check it out before rejecting it. I don't want to be narrow-minded.

Possible answers:

If I don't use the new procedure, I'm pretty sure my sales will fall off. "Using the new procedure could keep your sales high — or maybe push them even higher."

Using the new procedure will enable me to earn enough money to pay off my credit cards. I'm so sick of being in debt! "You like the idea that the new procedure will help you get out of debt, which is important to you."

Sticking with my old way is going to lead to trouble—some of my coworkers are already mad at me, and I hate that. "Using the new procedure is going to help you get along with your coworkers better and allow you to feel more comfortable with the group."

I like being one of the group, and everyone else is on board with this. I don't like being left out. "You like being part of the group. And using the new procedure means you can continue to feel that way. Using it allows you to overcome or avoid feeling left out."

If everyone else thinks this is a good idea, I owe it to myself to at least check it out before rejecting it. I don't want to be narrow-minded. "It's important to you to be open-minded, so you want to use the new procedure to make sure you've given it a fair shot."

RESPECTING AUTONOMY

One of the most common difficulties my trainees run into with action plans is resisting the urge to take over. They hold back during the Instant Influence conversation, they respect autonomy during the decision to create an action plan, and then comes the time to actually prepare the action plan and they can hold back no more. They know what needs to be done, they see someone doing it wrong, and they just can't help themselves—they have to interfere.

As one who has negotiated action plans with clients, colleagues, employees, patients in therapy, and family members, I'm sympathetic; believe me. It's difficult to watch someone doing something that you know isn't going to work. And, in fact, you don't have to sit on your hands or bite your tongue or stay out of the action plan completely. It will be helpful, however, if you continue to respect the autonomy of your influencee as the action plan is created.

What does this mean? Ideally, you will consider each part of the action plan and offer an autonomy-enhancing question about it:

- What might you want to choose as your target here?
- When do you want to have that done by?
- Tell me about the methods and strategies you might want to use.
- Why might you want to make this change at all?

You ask the question, she stays in charge of the process, and, as a result, she is as motivated as she can possibly be to implement the change and take ownership of the results.

On occasion, you may see a way to help or a part of the plan that needs to be modified. In such a case, ask permission before doing anything—and offer your suggestion only if you get the okay. If you don't, simply say that you'll be available if the influencee might want to ask you about it—if ever. (Those last two words are very important because they reemphasize your respect for the influencee's autonomy.)

Are you thinking, *I don't buy this. What if the other person puts all the wrong stuff in her action plan?* Yes, it's a worry and a possibility, but *not* one to be tackled during the first Instant Influence conversation. You've moved someone from a no to an action plan. That's a huge accomplishment. Don't risk ruining it by trying to micromanage your influencee's efforts to change. If the action plan focuses on one small step at a time with a relatively quick turnaround, you'll have plenty of opportunities to tweak the plan and offer help. Also, remember that when left to their own devices—and their own motives—people usually do a lot more than they specify in their action plan. They may even discover problems on their own and take steps to solve them.

TROUBLESHOOTING STRATEGIES

If someone resists creating an action plan...

- *Explain that the purpose of the action plan is to take you out of the equation and leave the process in his hands.* "I know this is *your* change. I think it would be helpful for you to write down exactly what you plan to do, because having your own record of what you decided will help you keep on track."
- *Reinforce the idea that it's effective to identify behavior.* "We've talked about a lot of different things just now. I think it might be helpful to write down the most important change, the one you really want to focus on."
- *Relate it to your own experience, if appropriate.* "I know that I've found it to be very helpful to make an action plan, because it clarifies exactly what I am going to do next, and when or how long I am going to do it. With that out of the way and written down, I almost don't have to think about it anymore."

- *Suggest it as an experiment.* "Would you be willing to give it a try, to see if you find it helpful in reinforcing your commitment to change?"
- *Remember that lack of a formal plan doesn't mean that he won't change.* It may be that he simply isn't ready to announce his intention to do something different.

If someone says no to an action plan...

- Keep in mind that your focus is on the *change,* not the action plan.
- Remember that strong commitment talk—a clear statement of commitment to a particular behavior within a specific time frame, with at least one genuine, personal reason—is the near-equivalent of a written action plan.
- Ask if you might memorialize the conversation in a memo that you will share.
- Express your intention to remember and return to the oral agreement: "I think we've come a long way. I'm going to make a note that you're working on this. Would it be okay if we check back in with each other next week?"
- Avoid threatening with consequences for not doing an action plan. Consequences should be imposed only for failing to do the behavior, not for failing to formalize it into a plan.
- Continue using the Instant Influence approach. Ask why the other person might want to make an action plan some other time.

If someone doesn't stick to an action plan...

- If you think the lapse is temporary, use the Instant Influence process to ask why the person might want to recommit to fulfilling the action plan.

- If you think the lapse is more serious, use an adaptation of Step 4 (Imagine you've changed. What would the positive outcomes be?) to ask what he thinks might happen if he doesn't implement the action plan. Make sure you inform him of any consequences.
- See chapter 10 to explore what to do if you determine the person probably won't change.

Most of the time, action plans work. But occasionally, of course, the best-laid plans simply don't go as we'd like. We make an effort—maybe even several efforts—but after days or weeks or months, the problem hasn't been solved, and by the looks of it, it won't be solved any time soon. To learn more about coping with this unhappy outcome, read on.

CHAPTER TEN

Moving On

You've done everything right, but change just isn't happening. Either the person you thought you had influenced isn't doing what she agreed to, or she never agreed to anything in the first place. Maybe you've endured several bitter fights, or days of icy silence, or tears and recriminations. Perhaps you've been met with a sunny smile and a nonchalant shrug, or a calm but firm admonition to mind your own business.

Or maybe you're the one who is failing to change. Maybe you've tried, but you haven't managed to take even the tiniest step toward the goal you said you wanted to achieve. Or you took the first step but not the second, or you took the second but stopped short of the third. You feel even worse than you did before you started the process, because now you haven't just avoided an action, you believe you've downright failed.

So what comes next? Here are a few suggestions:

- Accept the situation.
- Forgive yourself for not having complete control over it, or for maybe not having *any* control over it.

- Consider whether the Instant Influence process is simply taking longer to work than you had expected it to, with that "two steps forward, one step back" pattern that so often characterizes change.
- Consider whether the goal is simply the wrong one or whether there might be a different goal that is more appropriate and inspiring.
- Consider whether the goal is too ambitious and whether there might be a smaller, more manageable goal.
- Most important, whether you're the influencer or the influencee, ask yourself these questions:

   Why did I try to change this [or try to help someone change this] in the first place?
   Why am I upset about the absence of change?
   Why am I not prepared to let go of this goal?

Thinking about these questions may give you insight into the situation and help you realize what you can and cannot change. Then you can make a clear, informed decision about whether to continue the Instant Influence process or to accept that change just isn't going to take place.

Check Yourself

If you feel that an Instant Influence conversation hasn't worked, consider your role. Might you have been part of the problem? Did you...

- fail to reinforce the other person's autonomy?
- allow the focus to shift from "the reasons why you want to" to "the reasons why you don't want to, can't, or shouldn't"?
- allow the focus to shift from "why you want to" to "how it can or can't be done"?

- allow yourself to start answering the other person's questions rather than letting him find his own answers?
- try to help and make suggestions?
- slip into the tell-and-sell or high-threat approaches on occasion?
- choose a target behavior that was too ambitious, too modest, or not really a behavior but an attitude, a decision, or a result?
- forget the Dead Man's Rule and try to motivate a passive rather than an active behavior?
- get drawn into a discussion about anything other than why the person might want to do the chosen behavior?
- find yourself wanting the change for the other person more than he wants it for himself?
- miss any opportunities to reflect back change talk and commitment talk?

Speaking as a therapist, consultant, coach, trainer, and parent, I know how hard it can be to keep focused and stick to the Instant Influence format. If you realize that you slipped and fell away from the approach, take heart. You can try it again. You might begin the second conversation with an acknowledgment: "I realize that last time we talked, I got very caught up in my own reasons for why you should do [the target behavior], and I apologize for that. I genuinely want to hear the reasons why you might want to do it, and I'd appreciate it if you'd give me another chance at that conversation."

If Someone Refuses to Change

It can be tough to know how to respond when someone refuses to change. Following are some suggestions to help you handle this difficult situation.

When do you walk away?

- When they ask you to.
- When you've gotten good motivational statements but no commitment (leave well enough alone).

What do you say?

- Acknowledge any change that has taken place and the motivation that has been discovered.
- End on a positive note.

What do you say when the change they committed to didn't happen?

- "Why was it important to you to make that commitment?"
- "Tell me how you prepared yourself to make that change."
- "What might you want to do next time to be more successful? And why might you want to do that?"

What shouldn't you say when the change they committed to didn't happen?

- "What went wrong?"
- "Why didn't you even try?"

How do you accept the lack of change without agreeing with it?

- Allow yourself your own opinions about what you think the other person should do.
- Share your feelings and opinions as your responses: "I personally would love it if you would follow this procedure, but it's not my decision. It's up to you. However, the consequences for doing it and for not doing it remain unchanged."

ACTIVE ACCEPTANCE

Sometimes the Instant Influence process doesn't have a happy ending, or at least not one that you ever get to hear about. The stubborn employee resigns or is fired. The pet project doesn't get off the ground. Your loved one doesn't progress as you had hoped. How do you handle that?

First, remind yourself that you don't have the whole picture—you don't know what might be going on in the person's mind or what might happen in the long run. You may need to act now based on what you *can* see—terminating someone's employment, ending a relationship, or spelling out consequences for your child—but don't be discouraged. There may be more promising days ahead.

Second, be aware that reinforcing the other person's autonomy consistently until the end of the process could potentially spark an inspiration that might ignite months or even years later. Conversely, letting loose all your frustrations and suggesting that you know best could short-circuit a slow-moving change.

I like to think of this open-ended mind-set as *active acceptance,* in contrast to passive acceptance or resignation. Active acceptance doesn't mean that you have to like what you're accepting, or that you have to agree with it, or even that you have to think it's for the best. It simply means that you understand that you've reached the limit, at least for the time being, of what you're able or willing to do about a situation.

I have to take this approach in my work as an executive coach and as a therapist, husband, and father. When I feel that Instant Influence has failed with a recalcitrant executive who's still struggling with his difficulty delegating time-sensitive tasks, I might say to him, "Look, at this point, it doesn't matter what I think. This is *your* decision." But rarely do I mean,

"You're doing the right thing." Perhaps if I could make decisions for the executive, I might be tempted to do so; perhaps I would force him to delegate at the right times so he could see how much better his team would operate.

But whatever his decision, I have to accept it. I don't have to like it. I don't have to think it's for the best in some way I can't imagine—though sometimes, not always, I might get some comfort by telling myself that. And meanwhile, I need to think about my own limits and about what consequences might be best for him. I need to decide whether it's appropriate to continue coaching, whether I'm willing to invest more time in the process, whether it's in his interest for me to continue. Making that decision requires that I accept the limits of my control.

Active acceptance contrasts with resignation. To me, resignation implies, "This was my job to do, and I failed. I know exactly what terrible outcomes are awaiting my influencee, and I'm miserable about it." Active acceptance suggests, "This was never my responsibility. I was only trying to help someone else with *his* responsibility. Therefore, I didn't fail. And even if I think I know my influencee's fate, I don't, because the future is an unknown and people can really surprise us." I actively accept my influencee's right to make his own decisions, and I embrace my own ignorance of what the future might bring.

If we actively accept another person's decision not to change, what might the outcomes be?

• *We might be proven wrong in our predictions.* A colleague recently told me a moving story about how she had been absolutely certain that her elderly parents needed to move into an assisted-living facility before one of them died. "I don't see any way that the survivor will adapt to a move after that," she used to tell her friends. "If we can't get the move to happen soon, it's all over."

215

In fact, my colleague's father died before the couple moved, and her mother had to make the move on her own. As it happened, moving was just the activity her mother needed while coping with her beloved husband's death, and making new friends who had never known her as part of a couple actually made it easier for her to adjust to her new identity. "I couldn't have been more wrong," my colleague told me. "I really didn't want to admit it to anyone, but thank heavens my parents didn't listen to me!"

• *Left to his own devices, the other person may finally decide to make the change.* People often like the attention that comes from others being concerned about them. Without consciously realizing it, they refuse to change as long as people take an interest in helping them. When the "helpers" accept that change isn't going to happen, however, the attention stops and sometimes the change begins.

Likewise, people might refuse to change as part of a power struggle, no matter how supportive of their autonomy you may be. They define the change, even a change they've chosen, as somehow "giving in" to a parent, a boss, or an authority figure. And since preserving autonomy is more important to them than making the change, they dig in their heels and hold on to their old ways as long as they feel that they're locked in the struggle.

When the parent, boss, or authority figure genuinely backs off, actively accepting the person's refusal to change, the power struggle ends, allowing room for change to begin. Friends of mine struggled with their oldest son for years about homework. They fought bitterly over his study habits all through his junior-high and high-school years, until finally, in despair, they let him go off to college. They were certain that without constant monitoring, he'd flunk before the first semester ended.

To everyone's surprise, after a few weeks of floundering, the young man found his bearings and developed an interest in biology that he'd never shown in high school; he is now a thriving pre-med student. All he needed was his autonomy.

• *Things will continue as they have been or perhaps become worse, just as we predicted.* Perhaps the downward spiral continues, just as we knew it would. Perhaps the other person goes from bad to worse, exactly as we feared. Perhaps we were right, and the lack of change brings about the dire consequences we expected all along. What then?

Since we *don't* know what's going to happen, our manner of accepting another person's apparent failure makes a difference. If we're certain that his failure to change means inevitable doom, despair, and defeat, we will probably communicate that to him, which might make it even more difficult for him to change. The weight of our certainty that he can never change, coupled with his own fears and sorrows, may come to seem like an insuperable burden.

MOTIVATING YOURSELF TO ACCEPT AND ADAPT

Active acceptance has benefits for us as well. We can tell ourselves that the larger meaning and ultimate outcome of these events is beyond us. We should also tell ourselves that we did everything we could to improve the situation. We can impose the consequences that we've announced previously, secure in the knowledge that the other person is aware of them and perhaps even pleased that they are being meted out without aggression or hostility. Finally, we can work on actively accepting our own limits: what we can know, what we can do, what we can control.

Your final effort, then, is to motivate yourself to accept the situation and find a way to adapt to it. Naturally, your attempts to adapt will depend on the behavior of the person who isn't changing.

- *If you have gotten an absolute no:* Sometimes an absolute no can be the greatest gift of all, because it frees you from having to wonder what the situation really is. This no can take two forms: a verbal refusal to make the change you're asking for, or an action so egregious — cheating in a marriage, embezzling from a company — that it constitutes a de facto no.

- *If the person is asking for another chance:* In some cases, the person who isn't changing is unwilling or unable to accept his own lack of change. He wants another meeting, another heartfelt conversation, another action plan, anything other than what the situation really calls for: acceptance of his refusal to change. If your best judgment tells you that he's not likely to change, or if you're unwilling to give him another chance, *you* may be the one who needs to recognize the situation for what it is and refuse to participate any further. In doing so, you can still reinforce the other person's autonomy while stating your decision unambiguously:

> I've accepted that you're making your own choices here. But from my point of view, this is a no-go and we're not going to move forward. I think it's best that we don't talk about it again. I'm going to move on, and I wanted you to know that.

This is never an easy conversation to have. But if you find yourself struggling to end this interaction, that may be part of the problem: you may have wanted the other person to change more than he wanted to himself. We therapists are continually reminding each other never to be more invested in a client's change than the client is. This isn't an easy prescription to follow, especially for caring people. But it's crucial if you want to allow your colleagues and loved ones the autonomy they need to be in charge of their own process of change.

Struggling with Acceptance

If you're having a hard time accepting another person's inability or unwillingness to change:

- Remind yourself that this is his battle, not yours.
- Find a friend, colleague, or executive coach to whom you can safely vent. Express whatever urge you have to force, punish, cajole, or otherwise control the person who isn't changing. That way, you can avoid drawing on those feelings when you deal with him.
- Ask yourself what you've learned from this situation. If you would have done something differently, what would that have been?
- Shift the focus from the other person's need to change to your own need to accept.

CELEBRATING THE PROCESS

In my decades of doing this work, I've learned that the process of change is mysterious. We scientists study it, analyze it, and try to work with it as best as we can. But it unfolds in its own way and in its own time. Instant Influence is certainly the most effective system I've ever found for inspiring people to change.

In the end, though, the process works precisely because we aren't in control of it. Every person is responsible for his or her own change, and every person changes in his or her own way. Sometimes, our failure to change is a genuine failure. But sometimes, it's actually a powerful turning point that will lead to eventual success.

If you have participated in the Instant Influence process, congratulations. You've put your best intentions to work in the service of others. You've found a way to help your influencee— and perhaps even yourself—make a positive change. And that is always something to celebrate.

How I Finally Cleaned Out My Garage

I was working with a group of skeptical trainees—rehab counselors who were used to dealing with repeat offenders. They didn't believe that anything could motivate their clients to change. I tried to encourage them to find their own reasons for using Instant Influence, but they were having none of it. Finally one of them said to me, "Hey, Mike, how about we try this method on you?"

How could I refuse? The problem was, I had taught them too well. The task I picked for the exercise—cleaning out my garage—was one I had been avoiding for at least two years, maybe three, and it made me intensely uncomfortable to even think about. I don't know why I picked it—misguided dedication to the teaching process, no doubt—but suddenly I was being pressed by eager students who could see just how uneasy I was becoming.

"Okay, guys," I tried saying when they got to Step 3: Why didn't you pick a lower number? "I think you've got the idea."

No, they insisted. They wanted to try every one of the six steps, right to the very end. They kept asking me to complete

Step 5: Why are those outcomes important to you? Why did I want to clean out my garage?

It's probably an indication of how deep the issue went that I don't actually remember the reasons I gave, but here's what I do remember: when I got home that afternoon, somehow I started cleaning out my garage. My wife's sister was over for a barbecue, and she and my wife and I all started cleaning up together. The kids, who had been on a play date with friends, returned home and joined in. A chore that I had been dreading turned into a family celebration.

Now here's something even stranger: it didn't stop there. We went from cleaning out the garage to building one patio, then another. My wife's sister kept coming over to help out, and a couple of sets of neighbors did, too. All that summer, we were barbecuing and patio building several nights a week. It was like our own little block party, except at the end of the summer, I had a clean garage and two beautiful patios.

The depths of our influence can be mysterious indeed. Whether you use Instant Influence at home, at work, or out in the world; whether you use it with your colleagues, your employees, your loved ones, or yourself, there's one thing I guarantee: if you trust this process and allow it to run its course, you will be amazed where it takes you. I invite you to make the most of this process—and this book—as you continue your journey.

Acknowledgments

First and foremost, I acknowledge the love, support, and absolutely stellar professional guidance that my wife, Marianne Sharsky Pantalon, PhD, has given me over the past twenty-two years. I could never imagine a better partner in life or work. Thank you, Marianne—this never could have happened without you. I will love you forever. I also thank my older son, Matt, who at age four told me that, rather than flying all over the place to talk to people, I should "just send a book." Upon hearing that I didn't have one, he was stupefied and quickly replied, "Then write one—now!" Little did we know how long it would take and how much busier the process would make me. The book also would not have been possible without the ever-positive encouragement of my younger son, Nic, whose faith in me is similarly unyielding. He once told me, patting me gently on the back, "I'm going to get everyone to buy your book, Dad."

I would also like to thank my agent, Jeff Kleinman, for believing in me right from the very beginning, as well as for his brilliant and amazing help and reassurance during every step of the process. Huge thanks also to the whole team at Folio Literary Management, especially Celeste Fine and Molly Jaffa.

Collaborator Rachel Kranz, thank you for your stunningly impressive work throughout and for your extraordinary support, both in the writing process and for me personally as an author. Your ability to live and breathe the method, as well as your determination to get it just right, made you one of the best people to help give it life on the page.

Thanks as well to my editor at Little, Brown, Tracy Behar, for believing in this project and for her superior editing skills, which made the book a thousand times better than I ever could have imagined, and to Little, Brown executive vice president and publisher Michael Pietsch, to whom I will always be grateful. Much appreciation to the whole team at Little, Brown, especially Heather Fain, marketing director; Elizabeth Garriga and Laura Keefe, publicists; Christina Rodriguez, editorial assistant; Marie Salter, copyeditor; and Ploy Siripant, cover designer.

While the many people who have helped and supported me in developing the Instant Influence approach and in writing this book cannot all be mentioned here, I would like to recognize some extremely special ones who helped make the book what it is. Thanks to my best friend and adviser par excellence, Anthony Del Vecchio; and to my colleagues at Yale, especially Bruce J. Rounsaville, MD, Richard S. Schottenfeld, MD, David Fellin, MD, and Lisa Sanders, MD. Without the enormous help, clinical and research expertise, and brilliant mentorship of Gail D'Onofrio, as well as her unwavering faith in the approach, the research on which *Instant Influence* is based would never have existed; I am honored to be your colleague.

This book owes an enormous intellectual debt to William R. Miller, PhD, and Stephen Rollnick, PhD, for originating motivational interviewing, as well as for their generous and wise words of advice along the way. Their dedication and decades of hard work allowed a major shift in our ideas about what it means to motivate someone, bringing much-needed hope to the so-called impossible cases. I am humbled that they allowed me to take their work one step further.

Thanks also to Arthur J. Swanson, PhD, with whom I first evaluated the Instant Influence approach at St. Barnabas and Union Hospitals in the Bronx; Ruth Ann Harnisch, my business coach, without whom I would never have had the requisite "boldness" to do any of this; and the thousands of trainees who have listened to and loved my approach, shared their success stories, and provided extremely important feedback about what worked and what didn't, especially those at Yale School of Medicine's Departments of Psychiatry, Emergency Medicine, and Internal Medicine, and its Primary Care Residency Program, and at General Electric, Bristol-Myers Squibb, the State of Connecticut Judicial Branch's Court Support Services Division, Hazelden, and Community Solutions Incorporated of Connecticut.

My heartfelt thanks go to all of the people who read and gave very helpful feedback on earlier versions of the manuscript, especially Maurice Cayer, Manuel Paris, PhD, Melissa D. Fulgieri, PhD, Nancy Meyer Lustman, PhD, James Campbell, Jeffrey Barnes, Jenny Blake, Thomas Styron, PhD, Robert Bibbiani, Thomas Bavaro, Keith Furniss, Paula Calzetta, Brenda Westbury, Diane Barber, Natalie Travers, and Kerry Patterson. Enormous gratitude for the organizational skills of my current and recent research, administrative, and personal assistants, especially Meaghan Lavery, Carolyn Haller, and Tami Jahns. Thanks to all of my present and past students at Yale, especially Alia Crum, Madeleine Rafferty, and Michael Rodriguez, and for the moral support of family and friends, especially my parents, Mike and Nancy Pantalon; my brothers, Eddie and Jimi Pantalon; Ivan, Dana, Andrew, Tom, and John Drazic; John, Susan, Pamela, and Allison Bugden; Lisa Brandes, Laura Minor, William Carbone, Anne Vance, Stuart Sidle, PhD, David Tate, PhD, Ivka Osman, Casey and Leslie King, Jeff and Joan Campell, Carol Freidland, Rebecca Skloot, Rosemary

Jones, Thomas Crum, Robyn O'Brien, and Stephen Hinshaw, PhD. Appreciation to all of my coaching and therapy clients who taught me so much more than I taught them. And finally, thanks to the teachers who most influenced me: Robert W. Motta, PhD, Steve Fishman, PhD, Barry Lubetkin, PhD, and Richard Bentall, PhD.

I am eternally grateful to you all.

Notes

Introduction: Instant Influence in Action

1. Miller, W. R., & Rollnick, S. (1991). *Motivational interviewing: Preparing people to change addictive behavior.* New York: Guilford.
2. D'Onofrio, G. D., Pantalon, M. V., & Degutis, L. C., et al. (2005). Development and implementation of an emergency department practitioner-performed brief intervention for hazardous and harmful drinkers in the emergency department. *Academic Emergency Medicine, 12,* 211–218.
3. D'Onofrio, G. D., Pantalon, M. V., & Degutis, L. C., et al. (2005). Development and implementation of an emergency department practitioner-performed brief intervention for hazardous and harmful drinkers in the emergency department. *Academic Emergency Medicine, 12,* 211–218; Vasilaki, E., Hosier, S., & Cox, W. (2006). The efficacy of motivational interviewing as a brief intervention for excessive drinking: A meta-analytic review. *Alcohol and Alcoholism, 41,* 328–335; Martino, S., Haeseler, F., Belitsky, R., Pantalon, M. V., & Fortin, A. H. (2007). Teaching brief motivational interviewing to medical students. *Medical Education, 41,* 160–167; D'Onofrio, G., Pantalon, M. V., Degutis, L. C., Fiellin, D. A., Busch, S. H., Chawarski, M. C., & O'Connor, P. G. (under review). The brief negotiation interview reduces harmful and hazardous

drinking in emergency department patients; D'Onofrio, G., Pantalon, M. V., Degutis, L. C., Fiellin, D. A., Busch, S. H., Chawarski, M. C., & O'Connor, P. G. (2008). Brief intervention for harmful and hazardous drinkers in the emergency department. *Academic Emergency Medicine, 51,* 742–750.

4. Lundahl, B., & Burke, B. L. (2009). The effectiveness and applicability of motivational interviewing: A practice-friendly review of four meta-analyses. *Journal of Clinical Psychology, 65,* 1232–1245.

ONE. WHAT MAKES PEOPLE WANT TO CHANGE?

1. Brehm, S. S., & Brehm, J. W. (1981). *Psychological reactance: A theory of freedom and control.* New York: Academic Press; Seligman, M., Steen, T., Park, N., & Peterson, C. (2005). Positive psychology progress: Empirical validation of interventions. *American Psychologist, 60,* 410–421; Festinger, L. (1964). *Conflict, decision, and dissonance.* Palo Alto, CA: Stanford University Press. Bem, D. J., & McConnell, H. K. (1971). Testing the self-perception explanation of dissonance phenomena: On the salience of premanipulation attitudes. *Journal of Personality and Social Psychology, 14,* 23–31.

2. Brehm, J. W. (1966). *A theory of psychological reactance.* New York: Academic Press.

3. Scott, M., & Hale T. (2001). Psychological reactance: Evidence and theory. In J. P. Dillard & S. Hayes (Eds.), *Motivation and achievement: A reader.* New York: Guilford Press.

4. For a review of more such studies, see Burgoon, M., Alvaro, E., Grandpre, J., & Voulodakis, M. (2002). Revisiting the theory of psychological reactance: Communicating threats to attitudinal freedom. In J. P. Dillard & M. W. Pfau (Eds.), *The persuasion handbook: Developments in theory and practice* (pp. 213–232). Thousand Oaks, CA: Sage.

5. Worchel, S., & Brehm, J. (1971). Direct and implied social restoration of freedom. *Journal of Personality and Social Psychology, 18,* 294–304.

6. Dillard, J., & Shen, L. (2005). On the nature of reactance and its role in persuasive health communication. *Communication Monographs, 72,* 144–168.

7. Seligman, M., Steen, T., Park, N., & Peterson, C. (2005). Positive psychology progress: Empirical validation of interventions. *American Psychologist, 60,* 410–421.

8. Festinger, L. (1957). *A theory of cognitive dissonance.* Palo Alto, CA: Stanford University Press.

9. Bem, D. (1967). Self-perception: An alternative interpretation of cognitive dissonance phenomena. *Psychological Review, 74,* 183–200.

10. Pantalon, M. (1999). Motivational interviewing with dually diagnosed inpatients. In W. R. Miller, *Enhancing motivation for change in substance use disorder treatment: A treatment improvement protocol* (DHHS Publication No. SMA 99-3354) (p. 161). Washington, D.C.: Substance Abuse and Mental Health Services Administration (CSAT).

Two. Reinforcing Autonomy

1. Pantalon, M. V., & Swanson, A. (2003). Use of the University of Rhode Island change assessment to measure motivational readiness to change in psychiatric and dually diagnosed individuals. *Psychology of Addictive Behaviors, 17,* 91–97.

2. Pink, D. (2009). *Drive: The surprising truth about what motivates us.* New York: Riverhead Books.

3. Pantalon, M. V., Carroll, K., Nich, C., & Frankforter, T. (2002). Using the URICA as a measure of motivation to change among treatment-seeking individuals with concurrent alcohol and cocaine problems. *Psychology of Addictive Behaviors, 16,* 299–307; Carey, K., Maisto, S., Carey, M., Purnine, D. (2001). Measuring readiness-to-change substance misuse among psychiatric outpatients: I. Reliability and validity of self-report measures. *Journal of Studies on Alcohol, 16,* 79–88.

4. Deci, E. (with R. Flaste). (1995). *Why we do what we do: understanding self-motivation.* New York: Penguin.

5. Deci, E. (1972). Intrinsic motivation, extrinsic reinforcement, and inequity. *Journal of Personality and Social Psychology, 22,* 113–120.

6. Callahan, D. (2004). *The cheating culture: Why more Americans are doing wrong to get ahead.* Orlando, FL: Harcourt Books.

7. Rothman, A., & Salovey, P. (1997). Shaping perceptions to motivate healthy behaviour: The role of message framing. *Psychological Bulletin, 121,* 3–19.

THREE. THE SIX STEPS TO INSTANT INFLUENCE

1. Vaca, F. E., Winn, D., Anderson, C. L., Kim, D., Arcila, M. (in press). Feasibility of emergency department bilingual computerized alcohol screening, brief intervention and referral to treatment. *Substance Abuse.*
2. Pantalon, M. V., & Swanson, A. (2003). Use of the University of Rhode Island change assessment to measure motivational readiness to change in psychiatric and dually diagnosed individuals. *Psychology of Addictive Behaviors, 17,* 91–97.
3. Pantalon, M. V., & Swanson, A. (2003). Use of the University of Rhode Island change assessment to measure motivational readiness to change in psychiatric and dually diagnosed individuals. *Psychology of Addictive Behaviors, 17,* 91–97.
4. Pantalon, M. V., Carroll, K., Nich, C., & Frankforter, T. (2002). Using the URICA as a measure of motivation to change among treatment-seeking individuals with concurrent alcohol and cocaine problems. *Psychology of Addictive Behaviors, 16,* 299–307.
5. Carey, K., Maisto, S., Carey, M., & Purnine, D. (2001). Measuring readiness-to-change substance misuse among psychiatric outpatients: I. Reliability and validity of self-report measures. *Journal of Studies on Alcohol, 62,* 79–88.
6. Vasquez, N., & Buehler, R. (2007). Seeing future success: Does imagery perspective influence achievement and motivation? *Personality and Social Psychology Bulletin, 33,* 1392–1405.
7. Toll, B., O'Malley, S., Katulak, N., Wu, R., Dubin, J., Latimer, A., Meandzija, B., George, T., Jatlow, P., Cooney, J., & Salovey, P. (2007). Comparing gain- and loss-framed messages for smoking cessation with sustained-release bupropion: A randomized controlled trial. *Psychology of Addictive Behavior, 21,* 534–544.

Four. Influencing Yourself

1. Proulx, T., & Heine, S. (2009). Connections from Kafka: Exposure to meaning threats improves implicit learning of an artificial grammar. *Psychological Science, 20,* 1125–1131.

Six. Influencing People Who Don't Want to Change

1. Miller, W. Personal communication, April 11, 2003.

Eight. Identifying Change

1. Amrhein, P., Miller, W., Yahne, C., Palmer, M., & Fulcher, L. (2003). Client commitment language during motivational interviewing predicts drug use outcomes. *Journal of Consulting and Clinical Psychology, 71,* 862–878.

Nine. Making an Action Plan

1. Miller, W. R., Yahne, C. E., & Tonigan, J. S. (2003). Motivational interviewing in drug abuse services: A randomized trial. *Journal of Consulting and Clinical Psychology, 71,* 754–763; Amrhein, P. C., Miller, W. R., Yahne, C. E., Palmer, M., & Fulcher, L. (2003). Client commitment language during motivational interviewing predicts drug use outcomes. *Journal of Consulting and Clinical Psychology, 71,* 862–878.
2. Martino, S., Haeseler, F., Belitsky, R., Pantalon, M. V., & Fortin, A. H. (2007). Teaching brief motivational interviewing to medical students. *Medical Education, 41,* 160–167.
3. Linn, M., Lee, H., Tinker, R., Husic, F., & Chiu, J. (2006). Teaching and assessing knowledge integration in science. *Science, 313,* 1049–1050.
4. Gollwitzer, P. M., & Brandstaetter, V. (1997). Implementation intentions and effective goal pursuit. *Journal of Personality and Social Psychology, 73,* 186–199.
5. Locke, E. A., & Latham, G. P. (2002). Building a practically useful theory of goal setting and task motivation: A 35-year odyssey. *American Psychologist, 57,* 705–717.

Index

233

About the Author

Michael V. Pantalon, PhD, is an award-winning faculty member at Yale School of Medicine and maintains a practice as a motivational coach, consultant, speaker, and therapist. At Yale, Dr. Pantalon teaches undergraduate and graduate courses in personality psychology and the history of psychology; and classes at the medical school on clinical psychology and motivational interviewing. He and his colleagues conduct research on the effectiveness of his adaptation of motivational interviewing (the basis of *Instant Influence*) and substance abuse treatment in a variety of health-care and criminal justice settings, work that has received more than $22 million in federal funding over the past decade.

As a psychologist, Dr. Pantalon has devoted his career to researching Instant Influence and to teaching it to thousands of trainees. He has taught people from all walks of life: business executives, human resources managers, executive and lifestyle coaches, parents, teachers, sales representatives, probation officers, psychologists, and other health-care professionals, as well as to individuals struggling with a range of addictive and compulsive behaviors. He has consulted with businesses and organizations such as General Electric, Bristol-Myers Squibb, Schering-Plough, Crossroads at Antigua, Hazelden, the National

Institutes of Health, and the US Department of Health and Human Services, among many others.

Dr. Pantalon has published numerous articles on his research in publications such as the *New England Journal of Medicine* and the *Journal of the American Medical Association,* and has presented his work at national and international conferences. He earned his BA in Psychology from Binghamton University; his MA and PhD in Clinical and School Psychology from Hofstra University; and his MS in Clinical Psychopharmacology from the Massachusetts School of Professional Psychology. He lives in Hamden, Connecticut, with his wife, Marianne, and their sons, Matthew and Nicholas.

To learn more about Dr. Pantalon and his work, visit www.michaelpantalon.com.